Welcome
to
Psilocybin

An Easy Guide to Growing and Experiencing
the Potential of Magic Mushrooms

Seth Warner

Foreword by Dennis McKenna
Executive Editor Ed Rosenthal

QUICK
AMERICAN
PUBLISHING

WELCOME TO PSILOCYBIN:
An Easy Guide to Growing and Experiencing the Potential
of Magic Mushrooms

First Printing

Copyright © 2023 Seth Warner
Published by Quick American Publishing
A Division of Quick Trading Company
Piedmont, California, USA

ISBN: 9781936807574
eISBN: 9781936807581

Printed in USA

Executive Editor: Ed Rosenthal
Project Director: Jane Klein
Developmental Editor: Susan Lang
Production Editor: Jennifer Leo
Design: Scott Idleman: Blink Design
Cover Photography: Seth Warner
Interior Photography unless noted: Seth Warner

Contributors

Seth Warner, Author, is a community advocate and educator in the psychedelic space based in the San Francisco Bay Area. In 2018 he began his journey directing the San Francisco Psychedelic Society and by 2019 helped decriminalize psilocybin in the city of Oakland. Alongside his work with these initiatives, Seth began MycoRising to teach home-scale psilocybin cultivation and has taught thousands of new growers through his workshops and *Ready? Set. Grow!* online program. He now seeks to teach a broader audience while building community locally through initiatives such as Hikerodose Oakland.

Dennis McKenna, Foreword Author, is an ethnopharmacologist who has studied plant hallucinogens for over 40 years. He is the author of many scientific papers, and co-author, with his brother Terence McKenna, of *The Invisible Landscape: Mind, Hallucinogens, and the I Ching*, and *Psilocybin: Magic Mushroom Grower's Guide*. He is a founding board member of the Heffter Research Institute, a nonprofit organization focused on the investigation of the potential therapeutic uses of psychedelic medicines.

Ed Rosenthal, Executive Editor, is one of the world's leading experts on the cultivation of cannabis. His books have sold over two million copies and his recent edition of *Cannabis Grower's Handbook* has revolutionized the field. Beyond the garden, Ed has been active in promoting and developing policies of civil regulations for entheogens that enable adults to legally consume cannabis and psychedelic substances.

Premium Sponsor, Inoculate the World

Table of Contents

Foreword   **6**

It's a New Era!   **10**

A Brief History   **13**

The Legalization and Decriminalization Movement   **16**

The Global Distribution of Psilocybin Mushrooms   **18**

Psychedelics and Safety   **22**

What to Know about Dosing   **32**

Microdosing   **42**

Macrodosing   **52**

The Mushroom Life Cycle   **68**

The Cultivation Life Cycle   **72**

Keeping It Clean   **76**

Ready, Set, Grow!   **84**

Phase 1: Colonizing Precooked Rice Bags   **86**

Phase 2: Colonizing the Tub   **112**

Phase 3: Harvest, Storage, and Continued Maintenance   **132**

Scaling Up Options   **154**

Resources   **160**

Foreword

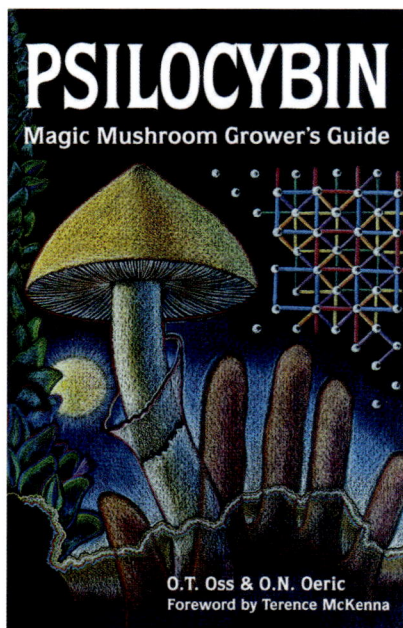

In 1975, my brother, Terence McKenna, and I published a little book entitled *Psilocybin: Magic Mushroom Grower's Guide.* We were concerned about potential legal repercussions for publishing such a subversive and obviously dangerous book, so we elected to publish under pseudonyms; O.N. Oeric was the one I chose, while Terence's was O.T. Oss. The book—really little more than a pamphlet—was published by a radical Berkeley publishing house, And/Or Press. It contained detailed instructions for growing small amounts of *Psilocybe cubensis* mushrooms in mason jars on a substrate of sterilized rye. Although the technique was simple, it did require a certain degree of focus and the ability to maintain a relatively sterile working environment. But anyone with a little patience could persist through one or two abortive attempts and eventually succeed in producing more than enough mushrooms for personal use with plenty left over to share with friends. Some people with more entrepreneurial aspirations established grow-ops of thousands of jars! While large-scale cultivation could be accomplished using this method, it was labor intensive, and most growers soon discovered better ways that were closer to conventional methods for growing edible mushrooms.

But at the time the book was published, growing methodologies were known only to a few fanatics. And they, perhaps concerned about competition, guarded their secret knowledge and did not readily share it. Terence and I, on the other hand, had a more messianic mindset and wanted to share our discoveries with the world. So our little book, PMMGG, became one of the first to be published that described growing techniques for psilocybin mushrooms that could be easily mastered by any relatively astute 11th grader. Clearly, there was an unmet demand, and this book fulfilled it. There were apparently legions of eager 11th graders and many others who were looking for something like this. Initial sales started out briskly, and the book has continued to sell steadily for nearly 50 years. It has gone through three different publishers and several editions, and has sold well over 100,000 copies.

But folks who enjoy growing mushrooms are hands-on by nature and inclination, and as a result, there has been a lot of innovation in this field in the last decades. One of the landmark publications was *The Mushroom Cultivator: A Practical Guide to Growing Mushrooms at Home*, co-authored by Paul Stamets and Jeff Chilton and published in 1983 by Agarikon Press. Nearly two decades later, in 2000, Paul Stamets published an even more comprehensive tome, *Growing Gourmet and Medicinal Mushrooms*, this time under the imprimatur of Ten Speed Press. Both of these publications were significant in that they provided methodologies applicable to a wide variety of psychedelic, medicinal, and edible mushrooms. They also marked a departure from the labor-intensive methods presented in PMMGG, which required a sterile working environment and was prone to contamination by molds and other unwelcome interlopers.

These new methods did not require total sterility and utilized composted substrates of horse or cow manure and straw, seeded by mycelium grown on sterile grain substrates. This was closer to conventional techniques of mushroom cultivation that have been widely used in the industry for years. But our little book, PMMGG, has held its own and continues to be a practical guide for growing small amounts of Psilocybe cubensis that can be readily adapted to small spaces, such as a spare closet or stairwell. It's proved to be particularly suitable, and in some cases an economic boon, for students living in cramped dorm spaces.

Now Seth Warner of MycoRising has produced the next iteration in this venerable legacy. His work, which you hold in your hands if you're reading this foreword, is entitled *Welcome to Psilocybin*; it's kind of a one-stop shop for aspiring mycologists and psilocybin enthusiasts. It incorporates a lot of ancillary materials that are not found in these earlier works, all of which were singularly focused on mushroom cultivation. This book certainly provides that. It contains detailed instructions on how to grow a mushroom mini-garden in a 6-quart tub that can easily fit on a bookshelf. So like PMMGG, it is suitable for those who may not have the space for a full-scale growing operation; yet it still affords a reliable way to produce more mushrooms than any one person could reasonably use in a year. It also includes instructions on how to create a liquid culture bank to preserve your favorite strains.

So, the book provides the basics on how to cultivate psilocybin mushrooms. But it doesn't stop there. It also provides context, with sections on the culture and history of magic mushrooms, a review of current psilocybin science, and a review of the current legal status of psilocybin and magic mushrooms.

The book also includes guidance on how to use psilocybin mushrooms for maximum benefit. It covers core concepts on how to create an optimal setting, and how to prepare for a psilocybin journey, how to navigate the dimensions it opens, and how to integrate the messages from the mushroom teachers.

There are also sections providing guidance on macrodosing and microdosing, with a description of best practices for a successful microdosing regimen.

In general, *Welcome to Psilocybin* will be a good handbook to have on hand, especially for those who are new to mushroom cultivation or just beginning to explore the wondrous world of psilocybin. It will also be useful to some who are well experienced with psilocybin and familiar with cultivation methods. It reflects the collective contributions of Seth and others in the mushroom community, all with experience in growing and using psilocybin mushrooms. Even if you're an "old hand," you're likely to learn something new from this book.

Dennis McKenna
Abbotsford, British Columbia
February 2023

It's a New Era!

A new era of magic mushroom cultivation has arrived: the third wave of what is still a relatively new practice, existing only since the mid 1970s. The first wave, spearheaded by the likes of Dennis and Terence McKenna, featured only one or two books and many more hurdles to overcome than we have today. The second wave was defined by the evolution of the internet, where more approachable methods such as Robert McPherson's PF Tek increased accessibility, and all varieties of growing methods were discussed, attempted, roasted, and refined in online forums like the Shroomery. This third wave magnifies the online cultivation community and access to information. Now you can hear the very first whispers of in-person mushroom cultivation groups and find a plethora of online shops that offer reliable, high-quality, and effective materials to mix and match and to fit together as pieces of a puzzle.

So if it's all become so easy, why write a book? This book is not here to make you a mycologist; let's get that out of the way. The biggest issue with the current state of mushroom cultivation is the number of methods, too many to count. And if you start looking around online, the term "rabbit hole" comes to mind. This book is not here to walk you through all your options. It is here to filter out almost all the options, leaving you a simple method of mushroom cultivation.

This book does have a technical edge, with new information, simplified and approachable—but the process is about something much greater than the accomplishment of a series of tasks. For the conscious cultivator, one who acts with intention and awareness, the cultivation of mushrooms becomes the catalyst for your relationship with mushrooms. The experience is more akin to taking in a new pet than simply growing some flowers or tomatoes. As you summon the mushrooms remember why you are bring-

Hillbilly ready to harvest

ing them forth and know they have the power to change your mind, in some cases forever. This relational element may prove to be a huge ally in whatever goal you are pursuing, whether simply a fun time or a profound redefinition of your purpose and path in the world. You decide.

Psychedelics are largely a psychological phenomenon. The concept of the relationship can help underpin a deeper sense of connection, affection, and respect for the mushroom. Many new seekers find themselves receiving mushrooms with a big question mark, not knowing what they have, where it came from, or how potent it may be. They often feel stress from the many hoops they jumped through and the risks they took to obtain the mushrooms. While you cannot and should not ignore the cultural taboo of these fungal beings, you can hold that shadow while inviting the light of conscious relationship in your pursuit of growth, healing, and perhaps joy. Stalling on the project, struggling to get it started is normal, but you should feel no shame or resistance in your pursuit. This book will guide you in unblocking and unlocking each step on your path toward cultivation of fungi and self.

Every subject covered in this book is just the beginning. All of it is simple data. None of it is the real thing. The predominant advice throughout is the one takeaway that really matters: start low and go slow, in both growing and using mushrooms. No two people's experiences are the same, so don't assume that all the information found in this book will be relevant to your own experience. I'm just presenting a general lay of the land, a way to get acquainted, hopefully a warm welcome.

It is fun to play up the excitement of our cultural moment with psilocybin and psychedelics at large, and throwing around terms like "magic" and "the medicine" makes everything seem light and positive. But please don't forget to balance all the positivity with a pause for gratitude and a grain of salt for the challenging truths of this time in human history. There is a lot of work to do, connections to build and rebuild. Thank you for taking a step toward greater knowledge of self, discovering new perspectives, and cultivating an intentional relationship with a powerful teacher in the form of the humble mushroom.

We are at the beginning of a new era, and we don't know what will come next. It is likely that the restriction of psilocybin will continue to fall away, but tight regulation is also a possibility. In either event, please don't break the law using the information in this book and please don't use mushrooms in a way that puts you or others at risk or in harm's way.

With any luck, the cultivation method in this book will remain relevant for years to come. But with a lot of luck, new advancements in both the use and cultivation of psilocybin will overtake this book sooner than later. Meanwhile, there is plenty more information in the world about all the subjects in this book, so please go forward, learn until you are full, give it some time to digest, learn a bit about yourself, and dig in once again!

Welcome to psilocybin.

A Brief History

The story of mushroom cultivation has a very long history, and the history of psilocybin use goes back far beyond our ability to record it. Luckily, the history of cultivating psilocybin-containing mushrooms indoors is mostly recent. Let's take a brief walk through the record of psilocybin in Western culture.

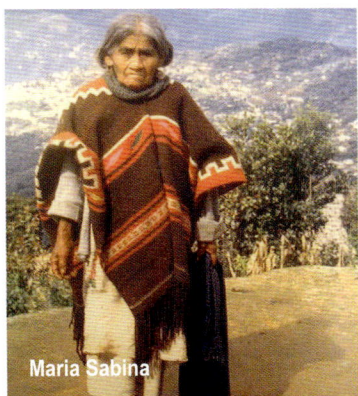
Maria Sabina

Maria Sabina

Maria Sabina (1894–1985) was a Mazatec curandera from a small village in Oaxaca, Mexico, who became known for her practice of using psilocybin mushrooms, which she called "little saints," in healing ceremonies. Living a traditional rural life in the Mazatec mountains, Sabina was born into a family of healers and introduced to the use of sacred mushrooms at a young age. As a curandera deeply respected within her community and surrounding villages, Sabina used many methods in her healing practice, including psilocybin mushrooms, which facilitated communication with the spiritual world to help heal the sick.

Sabina's life changed in 1955 when she was introduced to R. Gordon Wasson, an American banker and amateur mycologist who became the first Westerner to partake in a Mazatek ceremony involving psilocybin mushrooms. He published his account against Sabina's will and inadvertently launched her to international fame and brought a damaging wave of attention and tourism to her small village.

In some ways, Sabina's story is tragic. She lost her husband and two children, faced many challenges living in a remote village, and was then banished from her own village and even briefly jailed for her role in the surge of outside seekers who brought mass disruption with them.

Despite the immense challenges and tragedies, Sabina's enduring spirit and profound dedication to healing left a lasting legacy. Her pioneering work as a Mazatec curandera brought the therapeutic potential of psilocybin mushrooms to light, forever transforming our understanding of these sacred tools. Sabina's life also highlights the need to respect and preserve indigenous knowledge and traditions, and serves as a poignant reminder of the wisdom these cultures hold.

"Before Wasson, nobody took the children [the sacred mushrooms] simply to find God. They were always taken to cure the sick." – Maria Sabina

The McKenna Brothers

About 20 years after the publication of the Life article that revealed Maria Sabina, Terence and Dennis McKenna journeyed to the Colombian Amazon seeking another indigenous tradition, a hallucinogenic snuff called yopo. After giving up hope to find this substance, the team camped out and awoke in a field exploding with Psilocybe cubensis and soon consumed enough mushrooms to write vividly about their experiences: The Invisible Landscape by Terence and Dennis, and The Brotherhood of the Screaming Abyss by Dennis.

THE BROTHERHOOD OF THE SCREAMING ABYSS

MY LIFE WITH TERENCE MCKENNA

DENNIS MCKENNA
Foreword by Bruce Damer

Upon returning to the United States, Dennis developed a reliable method for cultivating P. cubensis that could be replicated outside the lab. It was an exhilarating adaptation of recent innovations in the world of mycology. Soon the brothers (under the pen names Oss and Oeric) published one of the first and best-known mushroom cultivation guides, *Psilocybin: Magic Mushroom Grower's Guide*. The book is still in

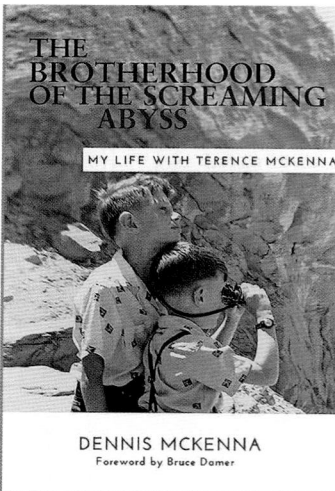

print, largely to mark a significant piece of history. The brothers launched a new era of democratized access to psilocybin, although their method was complex and required a high initial investment.

Internet Age, Professor Fanaticus

The initial success of the McKenna growing guide spurred interest, access, and experimentation just as internet use was becoming widespread. Various

websites and message boards popped up to share information. No contribution was more notable than that of the late Robert McPherson, aka Psilocybe Fanaticus, who put together the best of emergent techniques, referred to as teks. He created a method, PF Tek, that removed obstacles and increased the accessibility of psilocybin by several magnitudes. PF Tek's popularity is waning, as a variety of even simpler methods become available.

PF Tek uses small open mouth jars to create simple cakes that fruits as is in a humid environment. Photo by L.G Nicholas

Shroomery and Beyond

In the late 1990s, the shroomery.com became a new home for mycology online and since then has spawned more new growers than any other source. While not always an easy-to-navigate resource for new growers, it provides a home for ongoing discourse, an often-nurturing community for new experimentation, and a constant source for innovation. At its core, the shroomery has been a cultural catalyst, further democratizing mushroom cultivation.

The Legalization and Decriminalization Movement

Psilocybin exists in an unprecedented time of access, popularity, therapeutic potential, and medical intrigue. At the same time that you can buy this book, watch the docuseries *How to Change Your Mind*, and legally order mushroom spores to your home, it is still very possible to end up in the courthouse for pursuing the healing powers of fungi.

Cases such as that of an Indiana woman facing 10 years in prison and losing access to her children for growing mushrooms and microdosing are in no way common, but it's important to remember they are not impossible. Not long ago, the boundary was more obvious: mushrooms and psilocybin were illegal. With more and more states, counties, and cities passing legislation to deprioritize, decriminalize, or legalize psilocybin, people are left wondering what is legal or tolerated.

Today, the legislative landscape is increasingly dotted with safe havens and the media is painting the movement in a brilliant white healing light. Psilocybin and psychedelics tempt millions of people around the world who are seeking safe solutions for a variety of mental health and physical issues. Unfortunately, the speed of change is not orderly; it is a chaotic combination of hoping, healing, and navigating the laws and society's changing parameters.

Tread carefully and follow the law. There is an interesting, beautiful, and sometimes troublesome quality to new psychedelic explorers, who often feel it is their mission to pass on their experience to others, to save the world, or at least to save a friend or family member. Newcomers are well advised to let the "honeyshroom" period pass and to make sure their feet are firmly planted before preaching the mushroom gospel. It is not a rarity to meet someone who has landed in hot water for passionately or unwittingly announcing their new hobby.

Bills and Measures to Decriminalize Psilocybin

In March 2019, voters approved the Denver Psilocybin Mushroom Initiative, Ordinance 301, which kicked off the movement to decriminalize psilocybin. Voters there had approved cannabis decriminalization a few years earlier.

Very soon after, the Oakland, California, city council passed a measure that allows any growing, gathering, or gifting any naturally occurring psychedelic compound within the Oakland city limits. The Oakland ordinance regulates only the Oakland Police Department, but not other law enforcement agencies in the same jurisdiction, such as the California Highway Patrol and the Bay Area Rapid Transit (BART) police. The breadth of the ordinance has not been tested. However, unlicensed mushroom shops operate there without legal intervention. Although this situation is nothing to rely on, it seems quite rare that individuals growing and using mushrooms for personal use have any issue with the law.

Decriminalization Is Actually Deprioritization

The Oakland initiative, and many like it, do not exactly decriminalize psilocybin. Instead, they direct the relevant police department not to dedicate any city funds to the investigation, arrest, or prosecution related to growing, gathering, or gifting naturally occurring psychedelic compounds. This is not as reassuring as decriminalization would be, but, hopefully, these baby steps will inspire the next wave of initiatives and legislation that further increase our personal freedoms and cognitive liberty.

New legislation concerning psilocybin differs from one city or state to the next. For example, some statewide initiatives, such as Oregon's decriminalization of mushrooms, permit so small a quantity that it can never apply to cultivation; you would have to pick only a very small quantity of mushrooms in the wild to avoid breaking the law. Pay close attention to your local laws.

The Global Distribution of Psilocybin Mushrooms

It is quite common to think that magic mushrooms are just one thing, but mushrooms referred to as "magic" are far from identical. Psilocybin is found in a wide variety of mushrooms. The most common species among growers and consumers is *Psilocybe* cubensis; however, the genus Psilocybe contains more than 100 species. Beyond that genus are more than 100 other species, all containing some level of psilocybin.

Just because a species contains psilocybin does not mean that it is a choice psychedelic. Most of these species are not typically used: many are found only in the wild, some are rare, most are not easily grown, others are not very potent, and some are so tiny that it would take a very long time to collect enough.

Photo by L.G Nicholas

Psilocybin-containing fungi pop up all over the globe, but, like fungi generally, they have not been well studied due to their ephemeral nature. It is only more recently that the kingdom of fungi is beginning to gain the attention that it deserves. New species of psilocybin-containing mushrooms are regularly being discovered, and mushroom cultivators are pushing the limits on what can be grown at home. While this book maintains a narrow focus, there is far more to this hobby, or obsession, than meets the eye of casual new growers.

Focus on *Psilocybe Cubensis*

Psilocybe cubensis grows very well on cow poop and the poop of many other grazing animals. This means that in hot, humid places with grazers, P. cubensis is likely to be working the land. Northern California, where I am located, is a bit too dry for this kind of environmental stimulus; however, more southerly states and much of Florida have long-standing traditions of farmers chasing teenagers off their dairy or cattle farms.

Outside the farm, P. cubensis is easily the most commonly grown magic mushroom. It is likely that 90 to 99 percent of all home mushroom grows are P. cubensis. There are two probable reasons that this species is synonymous with mushroom cultivation. The clearest is that it is an incredibly easy mushroom to grow. The second is that it has a long track record of use and was probably the first psychedelic mushroom ever cultivated indoors. Since then, many varieties of P. cubensis have have been bred.

At first, most strains were gathered throughout the world and carried the name of their origins, such as Thai, Burma, Ecuadorian, and Amazonian. Just as with cannabis, these landrace, or original, strains were bred as growers selected, refined, and redefined them. Similarly, all cannabis comes from just one species, Cannabis sativa, which has been bred into a huge variety of strains with many different appearances and effects. While analytical research with cannabis is quite advanced at this time, the description of the many compounds in mushrooms and their effects on cognition is only just beginning.

There is a saying in the world of *P. cubensis* cultivators, "A cube is a cube"—meaning that without the experience and discernment of a real connoisseur, the main difference noticeable from one cubensis mushroom to another is potency. But things are changing, and lab testing is beginning to tell a bigger story. The simple takeaway is that, yes, there are differences from one variety to the next, but it is ultimately the combination of that mushroom and your unique physiology and psychology that will dictate the experience at hand. So be careful not to expect your experience to be the same as another person's. Beyond P. cubensis, there are very real differences from one species to another, from P. zapotecorum, sometimes reported as similar to an extended trip on the hallucinogenic DMT, to P. azurescense, well known for its paralyzing effect on the body. The large majority of these exotic species can be expected to remain unavailable to the average consumer for a long time to come.

Today, there are hundreds and perhaps thousands of individually isolated phenotypes (strains) of *P. cubensis*. Just as there are location-dependent varieties, a wide variety of names and expressions have resulted from cultivators making very intentional selections for specific traits, such as potency, color, size, and flush consistency. Frequently, the name has little to do with the actual expression of genetics, but not always.

Standard Strains: Golden Teacher, B+, AA+, Amazonian, Cambodian, Mazatapec

When it comes to finding the right strain, there is a much longer list of potential options to start with—but the names listed here fill the niche of great mushrooms for first timers to grow. These varieties have become standards in the community because they have been around for a long time and produce reliable flushes in a variety of conditions.

While there are differences in how these mushrooms grow, all of the varieties listed will be good choices for your first experience. Most first timers go with one of the most common starter strains, but you can pick from a wider variety of strains based on what sounds, looks, and feels attractive to you. Just be sure to read the descriptions and make sure there isn't anything too exotic about your first choice. An increasing number of strange varieties are being grown for very high potency or other mutations that may affect growth habits and ease of cultivation.

Potent Mutants: Penis Envy, Enigma

Some varieties have been bred and selected for unique traits or interesting mutations. One of the first mutant varieties is Penis Envy and its family of similar strains, which typically have higher than average potency but take longer to mature and can trend toward smaller flushes. The strain called Enigma looks more like coral than a standard mushroom and has an odd growth habit and low yield, but is capable of very high potency and stands out for its overall strange appearance. Mutants are not necessarily more difficult to grow, although they can be, but they require more patience and their effects may be very powerful. Keep in mind that more potent does not equal better. Many people intentionally avoid these strains due to the intense and challenging experiences they are more likely to produce.

Psychedelics and Safety

The Feeling of Mushrooms

Copious depictions of what it is like to ingest psilocybin appear in the media. Despite the many artful and inspired ways to describe an individual experience, ultimately they always fall short of the experience itself. More importantly, the experiences you read about are not very likely to inform you specifically about the experience you are going to have. Although there is no way to understand the experience until you have had it, perhaps the following will describe it in a general way that won't create too many expectations.

The use of psilocybin is commonly depicted as a visual phenomenon, but in reality the experience extends to all the senses in subtle and not-so-subtle ways. For most users, the greatest initial impact is the intensification of feelings, more so on the emotional side than the physical. While diversity of experience is the norm, imagine that all five senses, or perhaps six senses, are connected to a central control panel adorned with just a single knob and labeled "sensitivity." The use of psilocybin, and other psychedelics for that matter, can be reliably understood as turning that knob up and increasing overall sensitivity. The size of the dose and attention to preparation will ultimately have a lot to do with how far the knob gets turned. Hopefully, this little visualization provides context to perhaps the best generalization of psychedelics at large: nonspecific amplifiers.

It is through this increased sensitivity that you can see beyond the walls and defenses that protect you from the outer world's harsh energy as well as your innermost critics. With this sight comes the opportunity to embrace a heightened awareness of self; it also presents the opportunity to tuck your tail between our legs and try to run. It is just as capable of enhancing the felt experience of love, joy, and wholeness, but in the end it is the combination of what resides within your very own consciousness and your surroundings that is then served up for amplification when using psilocybin.

The self can be reliably compared to an antenna picking up a vast quantity of information from the inner and outer world all the time. It has been said that the brain's greatest function may be as a filter as opposed to a generator. Ultimately, there would be no way for our species to survive if it was weighed down by the constant barrage of sensory data. The brain helps filter out the unnecessary and keeps the antenna tuned to just the right volume for the needs of day-to-day life. Psilocybin can help consciousness move beyond basic survival as it temporarily loosens the filter and allows for a taste of a greater range of sensory experience and the development of new realization. Through the process of integration, new sensory experience and awareness can be grounded into the self and lead to a cascade of benefits, such as increased emotional intelligence, better stress management, greater alignment with goals and values, ease of communication, deepened relationships, and self-acceptance.

For many of us, our antennas have been tuned down to make way for the hustle and bustle of daily life in the modern age, and turning up the intensity should not be taken lightly. Learning to navigate states of heightened sensitivity is not the easiest skill to become aware of, let alone master. However, an increasing mastery of this skill should generally lead to a greater mastery of self through the core skill of increased self-awareness.

The psilocybin experience is only temporary and fades like a dream, unless you find some way to capture realizations and memories and integrate them into daily life. Hallucinations can take many forms, from open eye tracers across your vision to closed eye visuals that drop your consciousness into a formless hologram of intelligent light and vibrating fractal patterns, and well beyond that. Many things are possible, but few are typical; variety is the norm.

The following sections are intended to bring some clarity to safety essentials and sum up the variety of factors that influence a journey and how to work with them intentionally to craft the experience of your choosing.

Mushroom Safety

Are mushrooms safe? This question is no different than, Are knives safe? Knives can be safe, but they can also be dangerous, and they are certainly very useful; it is a matter of if, when, and how they are used. But what about mushrooms—should you use them, and if you do, how can you be as safe as possible?

Should You Use Mushrooms? Should You Avoid Them?

Some people should not use mind-altering substances of any kind, psilocybin included. If you have been diagnosed with or have a family history of schizophrenia, borderline personality disorder, or other serious psychiatric conditions, then it is best to avoid psilocybin completely. About 5 to 10 percent of the population falls into this category, and although many people don't have lifelong conditions to be concerned about, almost anyone can find themselves in the midst of deep stress and existential crisis. While psilocybin may be an enticing opportunity to break through such challenges, it is just as likely to magnify those challenges and even distance the user from that eventual breakthrough; the exercise of greater caution is advised. Adventuring into the realms of psilocybin is best done from a solid foundation. If your grip on reality is feeling a little slippery already, it is best to do more baseline housekeeping before delving further into the unknown.

A serious heart condition is another good reason to avoid psilocybin because of the potential for high highs that could spike blood pressure. If none of that applies to you and you're intrigued (after all, you are reading this book), then only you can decide if and when you're ready to use mushrooms.

What about Drug Combinations?

New explorers are advised to avoid combining psilocybin with other mind-altering substances, such as cannabis or other psychedelics, as they frequently have an amplifying effect that can be difficult to anticipate. For those with a little bit of experience, these combinations can be a ripe place for careful experimentation.

Pharmaceutical substances in combination with psilocybin can have a variety of impacts; much of the information is anecdotal because there has been almost no scientific research to date. According to such anecdotal reports, lithium and tramadol are among the very few pharmaceuticals reported to have caused harmful reactions, such as seizures, when combined with psilocybin. It's not a good idea to combine psilocybin with a newly prescribed pharmaceutical; allow plenty of time to see how you react to the medication. There's not enough room here to go into every drug combination, so do your own research.

A long-held misconception deems that taking psilocybin while on antidepressants (SSRIs, SNRIs, and MAOIs) can cause serotonin syndrome, or elevated levels of the neurotransmitter serotonin, with potentially serious consequences in certain cases. Cases of serotonin syndrome with psilocybin and pharmaceutical medication are incredibly rare. That said, the risk of serotonin syndrome is technically increased and the additional use of plant-based MAOIs, such as Syrian rue or caapi vine, should be avoided. Anecdotal reports say the combination of psilocybin and antidepressant is not a danger.

One effect of antidepressants combined with psilocybin that rings true is a general dampening of impact. For example, this could mean that the mushrooms might be only half as potent. Options are to use more psilocybin, to slowly reduce the intake of antidepressants over an extended period prior to using psilocybin, or to apply some combination of the two strategies. Anyone making this decision alone should do so cautiously and move forward using baby steps. Research terms like "tapering," "weaning," and

Typical Clinical Protocol

- The participant begins a series of psilocybin-assisted therapy sessions with either one or two therapists present. Typically, there are at least three sessions that focus on building trust, setting goals, addressing expectations, and preparing for the psilocybin experience.
- The psilocybin session takes place in a pleasant room with cozy furniture with one or two clinicians present. The patient is encouraged to find a comfortable sitting or lying posture and put on an eye mask to block out any visual stimuli and encourage an inward journey.
- Rather than taking mushrooms, the patient is administered synthetic psilocybin made in a lab. A dose between 10 and 35 mg is given at the beginning of the session; this quantity of manufactured psilocybin is equivalent to 1 to 5 grams of psilocybin-containing mushrooms. Throughout the session, the patient is usually left alone, although support is available if needed.
- If necessary, the clinicians work to return the patient to their internal experience by eliciting a sense of curiosity about what is happening. The intention is to be nondirective.
- The dose effect lasts 4 to 6 hours while the overall session generally lasts around 8 hours.
- After the session, the integration process begins with more talk therapy, processing the experience.
- In the days and weeks after the session, another two or three integration sessions are standard. These sessions typically focus on finding meaning in the psilocybin experience.

"titrating off" antidepressants, even if you don't plan to go fully off the medication. Making the decision with a prescribing physician, therapist, guide, or other support system is better yet. Keep in mind that while a dampened effect may be the norm, it may not be predictable or reliable, so starting off with standard dosing practices is advised before trying to make up the expected difference.

Psilocybin-Assisted Therapy

Much of today's excitement about the benefits of psilocybin has to do with psychedelic-assisted psychotherapy, which uses highly regulated protocols in a clinical setting to achieve a specific therapeutic affect. People may hear about the incredible results of these studies and think to themselves, I should do mushrooms, all the while missing the therapeutic focus. Mushrooms are likened to medicine, and consuming them is compared to therapy, but assisted therapy is different from just eating mushrooms on your own. Hopefully, this book can guide you to an experience that approximates the therapeutic approach, that it can help you build your own therapeutic support and make the most of your journey.

Finding Support

You could go solo on your journey, but keep in mind that uninterrupted time alone can be great medicine for one person and anxiety provoking for the next. Perhaps the edge of your comfort zone is exactly where you should be for personal growth, but if it holds you back, then options for support are available. Although support may be more relevant to macrodosing, still it's good to know what's available as you enter this new world of experiences.

Free Services

As the culture grows, so does accessible support. Here are some of the best services available for finding support from psychedelic, drug-related, and general harm reduction advocates.

Hotlines

The Fireside Project is found online at firesideproject.org, on the phone at 62-FIRESIDE (623-473-7433), or through the Fireside Project app. The app is the easiest method of contact, so consider downloading it prior to journeying. Fireside provides a volunteer lead hotline specifically for psychedelic support and post-journey integration. Volunteers complete a basic training and are often well versed in the skills of psychedelic support in their own life path prior to their work with the project.

Warmline.org provides an aggregated list of U.S.-based noncrisis phone lines for support of all kinds. The term "warmline" simply refers to the less heated nature of the calls the organization expects to receive.

988 is the phone number of the National Institute of Mental Health that can be called anytime to reach a support professional for suicidal ideation and any other type of mental health crisis. While the focus is on crises, anyone is welcome to call for any kind of support.

741-741 is a text-based 24/7 hotline. Upon receiving a text, a volunteer crisis counselor replies immediately with further resources and doesn't take long to follow up with a dedicated care provider. Like the National Institute of Mental Health, this hotline specializes in crisis intervention but is available for any type of support.

Community Organizations

All over the world is a (mycelial) network of community organizations dedicated to bringing together an otherwise disparate group of seekers, explorers, and healers. Many organizations have adopted the moniker of psychedelic society or club. A wide variety of groups exists outside of that naming template, and a great place to start searching for an in-person community is globalpsychedelicsociety.org (Global Psychedelic Society) for a global directory of psychedelic organizations. Many provide semiregular meetups or integration circles. Although these organizations don't often present themselves for the use of psychedelics, they are great places to connect with community, make new friends, and find support.

Sitter

A sitter is typically a peer oriented toward being present with you during a journey and offering simple support. This is a good option if you want a safety backup and perhaps someone to process your journey with afterward. In general, a sitter is advised to do little more than be present, listen, support you in simple tasks like a walk to the bathroom, and take notes of what you share to create a breadcrumb trail for later processing. A sitter does not require any specific training, but it is best to select someone with a high level of emotional understanding, a basic awareness of how they take up space, respect for you, and the willingness to let your process unfold without judging it. Said simply, a good sitter is a good listener.

Guide

A guide is a professional who may do similar work as a sitter in addition to providing more feedback or support, and pulling on certain threads when the moment seems correct. A guide should be expected to work with you in the preparation and integration phases of the experience. Here are important qualities to consider when choosing a guide.

Do they request an intake? An intake should be a lengthy form that provides an extensive background of medical and life history, which serves equally as an opportunity for the guide to know how to serve you as it does for you to take a full inventory of what you are bringing to the journey. It may take an hour or two to fill out the form.

Do they prioritize preparation and integration? Preparation is typically at least 2 hours of work that involves getting to know one another as well as setting intentions for the journey. Integration should be similarly prioritized to help you get grounded in the days and weeks after the session and make the most of your experience. Failure to prioritize integration is a red flag. (See Integration in the Macrodosing section.)

Are they willing to refer you to other guides? A guide's ability and desire to help you find the right fit is a good sign that their priority is focused more on your healing than their own business interest. It is also a signal that they are connected to a community of guides, increasing their likelihood of accountability and desire to preserve their integrity.

What is their policy on touch and consent in the psychedelic space? When it comes to touch, things can get touchy; parts of yourself can emerge unexpectedly, and suppressed urges can manifest into requests. If boundaries are unclear, then something normally unwanted can emerge only to be regretted once you are sober again. Understand that you might be the "irresponsible" party when it comes to touch and that any serious guide should have a lot to say about boundaries. Hand holding and similar reassuring touch are commonly allowed when you request it. Just be sure to get ahead of these potentials so you know with certainty that the space being held for you is truly safe.

Are they accountable to a larger community of practitioners? Most guides, though not all, have been a part of a training program or several training programs and may hold professional credentials as a therapist or a licensed social worker. A guide should at least be part of a larger community of people doing this work, even if just a single mentor. It may be hard to track actual connections, but listen to how they respond and speak about their community.

Are they representative of a cultural background that relates to your needs or preferences? In the highly awakened and sensitive state experienced in a journey, you become vulnerable, and the subtle energies of a guide can impact you so much more. Minor transgressions or simple "vibes" can get in the way of deepening and surrender. With this in mind, look for someone who best fits your idea of safety; this may be reflected in the practitioner's race, spirituality or religion, or gender identity.

Are they open to being interviewed by you? When you start asking questions and expressing your needs, how do they respond? Are they taking you seriously and to heart? If you don't love their vibe while you're sober, don't expect that to change once the medicine kicks in.

How to Find a Guide

Finding a guide is not always easy. Even in the San Francisco Bay Area, with the world's highest concentration of guides, people commonly do not to know how to find a way in. Try to meet people and make friends at psychedelic-friendly or -oriented events. Simply asking around is the best way to find local practitioners. Many cities have substance-free psychedelic-oriented gatherings organized by psychedelic societies and similarly identified groups.

For anyone unable to attend events in person, online events may help—although many stipulate not using the space to source medicine or guides. In that case, building relationships is the best hope. Finally, consider looking for integration specialists or finding therapists who list integration as part of their work. This won't always mean psychedelic integration, but reaching out for referrals is worth a try.

Integration Specialists

An increasing number of coaches and therapists focus on supporting people in the phases of preparation and integration of psychedelic experiences. Consider working with the support of a specialist when attempting to break through significant traumas or simply if the idea of the extra support is enticing.

These services can often be discovered through online directories:
- integration.maps.org
- psychedelic.support
- psychedelicaccessdirectory.com

What to Know about Dosing

The conversation about how much to take is increasingly broad reaching. For a long time, Terence McKenna's philosophy of 5 dried grams in silent darkness ruled the day. In the early 2000s, 3.5 grams was considered a dose. More recently, the advised introductory recreational dose was closer to 2.5 grams, and the museum dose around 1 gram. Then microdosing—just 0.1 gram (100 mg)—planted its flag. There are even a few advocates who favor high doses of 10 grams, 20 grams, 30 grams and beyond. However, the best advice, coming from high-dose advocates as much as anyone, is to start low and go slow.

Mushrooms Are Tools

Mushrooms, and psychedelics generally, are often described as tools. The question is, Are they staple guns or cannons, hammers or wrecking balls? It depends on how much you take. Mushrooms have the potential to stitch you back together and build you up, but they also have the power to blast you into the cosmos or shatter your reality. Dose, as well as setting and mindset, are among the factors that determine how these tools will impact you. The outcome is not as closely related to the inputs as you may be tempted to expect.

By building an intentional relationship with these substances and, when possible, with a specific strain of mushrooms, you have a better chance of aligning your expectations with your reality. Starting low and going slow is the key to building this relationship, dipping your toes into unknown waters, and beginning to understand your own personal experience when it meets psilocybin.

Dosing Guidelines

Dosing guidelines are just that, guidelines. There is a lot of variation from strain to strain and from batch to batch. Growing your own mushrooms will allow you to better know what to expect and ultimately make the best use of incrementally larger doses until you find your sweet spot. The basic dosing guidelines provide a general touchstone, but further refinement is needed to find the sweet spot—a term most relevant to microdosing, although it can also be applied to larger doses. Your personal sweet spot is dependent on strain, batch, freshness, and quality of the mushrooms. Many people amplify the message that a microdose of mushrooms is 0.1 gram (100 mg), but the truth is that often a microdose is around that amount. For the best results, you'll want to fine-tune.

Beyond being strain dependent, your microdosing sweet spot will be activity dependent. What is the right dose for a hike in the woods or some intense cardio? What is the best dose for meditative introspection and journaling? What is the sweet spot for a night out with friends?

When it comes to larger doses, the sweet spot has a lot to do with your comfort zone and desired outcome. Newcomers may be told to take exactly 3.5 grams, but that's a little bit like saying that a drink consists of three shots of whisky. Sure you can go that hard, but wouldn't it make more sense to try one shot before progressing?

With a consistent supply of mushrooms, weighing the dose is most helpful. However, consuming 1 gram of one strain of mushroom will generally yield different results than the same amount of another strain, although perhaps not vastly different. Keep this in mind as you try different strains.

In the future, advances in potency testing may make it possible and even easy to understand dosing based on psilocybin content. The current state of affairs is akin to treating all beers the same; the newcomer sees mushrooms in grams or milligrams, not considering potency. With alcohol, it is often second nature to know the difference between a refreshing lager or a heavy-hitting IPA.

Test Kits

Kits are available for testing mushroom potency, most notably the Psilo-Q test kit from Miraculix and Felix Blei, a chemist and harm reduction advocate based in Germany. These kits use a colorimetric scale to make evaluation simple, although determining the exact number can be tricky. The best use of these kits is for a rough estimate of potency as low, average, or high. While greater accuracy is technically available, it can be laborious to achieve.

Initially, potency information will have little meaning until you have had enough experience to relate number to impact. In clinical trials, 10 mg of psilocybin is considered a low dose, 20 mg an average dose, and 30 to 35 mg a high dose. If a sample tests for approximately 1 percent psilocybin, then you'll know that each gram (1,000 mg) of mushroom contains approximately 10 mg of psilocybin. These kits are available in the United States at qtests.org.

Microdose 0.05 to 0.25 gram (50 to 250 mg). Understood as a subperceptual or subthreshold dose, the microdose is one of the most popular ways to use mushrooms, as it often provides some or significant value without getting in the way of everyday activities. This dosing range is explored more thoroughly in its own section entitled Microdosing.

Minidose or threshold dose 0.3 to 1 gram This dosing range is less a term of use and more an awareness around microdosing and small doses. It describes the point at which you no longer feel quite like yourself. Your mushroom experience is heightened to a level that your actions and reactions begin to stray from your normal waking consciousness. The microdose exists below this threshold, and the museum dose typically exists at or above this dose. For new users, this dose can come with some anxiety, so give yourself plenty of time when playing around at this range.

Museum or small dose 0.5 to 2 grams. This dosing range is typically used by people who want to enhance another experience, such as going to a museum, attending a concert, hanging out with friends around a campfire, or hiking in the woods. The preferred practice in this range is to dose above the minidose or threshold level, to really feel the psilocybin, but to avoid the loss of normal functionality like walking, talking, and making rational decisions. This range can be the riskiest if you have a false sense of security and confidence that you are not taking "too much," when the actual effect can be intense. In exploring the world, you may find the unexpected to be overwhelming and even normal experiences can become unexpected emotional or irrational triggers. Be careful.

Macrodose 2 to 5 grams. This dosing range describes the most common method of ingesting mushrooms. It is the experience most people describe when saying they "tripped," "went on a journey," or simply "did mushrooms." This is also the most common range used for therapeutic benefit outside clinical trials. For details on this dosing range, see the Macrodosing section.

Heroic dose 5 grams. The heroic dose is more a number than an experience, but you can assume that this amount of mushrooms will be very intense. Whether or not it really is that intense depends on the potency of the mushrooms, but the general idea is that it will be a big trip. This dose should be approached with the same care and intent as any macrodose experience.

High dose 5 to 20+ grams. Beyond the heroic dose is a range that is more often discussed than experienced. There is a certain fascination with the very high dose experience. Even though it would be essentially impossible to eat enough mushrooms to die, there is the constant question of what would happen if you just ate a little more. Some people believe this is how

Factors beyond Potency: A Personal Story

I have experienced macrodoses of mushrooms numerous times, experienced several heroic doses, and played with the edge of high doses. The most visual journey I have ever had was with only 3.5 grams of mushrooms. I felt as though my conscious mind had been abducted from my body, moving through a wide variety of realms that can best be described as conscious, intelligent light. I went through many iterations of visual phenomenon, seeing what felt like the center of all creation, seeing myself as a baby tadpole developing in infinite tiny sacks lining the walls of a cavernous abyss, and so on. This experience came to me on a mushroom retreat after about 3 days of very intentional preparation including a clean vegetarian diet, yogic practices, and breathwork. I should also mention that the 3.5 grams were mixed into a full mug of thick cacao, sometimes used to enhance the power of the mushroom experience.

Besides the unexpected nature of the journey itself, I was just as surprised to find out that no one else out of about 15 people had had a similar experience despite having the same preparation and in many cases a similar dose. The point of this story? Potency isn't the only factor. Mushrooms are not known for consistency, and preparation can make a big difference. My best advice to you is to start low and go slow.

mushrooms are supposed to be used, and there is no doubt that higher doses provide unique and spiritually or existentially provoking experiences. There is also the reality that our culture has very little space for these kinds of experiences to be discussed, explored, or appreciated. Those who push this boundary often do so alone and can experience a heightened sense of alienation afterward. Great caution is advised when navigating higher doses, and certainly it is not for novices. Even staunch advocates recommend slow incremental progress into these higher realms with long stretches of time between experiences.

Logistics of Dosing

How to consume the mushrooms may be an even bigger question than the quantity of mushrooms to be ingested. The fork in the road leads toward whole fruit in one direction and simple extracts in the other.

Whole Dried or Fresh Mushrooms

Eating dried mushrooms is the most common way of using psilocybin. Typically, psilocybin-containing mushrooms are consumed dehydrated in their raw form. Dried mushrooms have the advantage of a long storage life, much longer than that of fresh mushrooms, which will keep in the refrigerator for 7 to 10 days.

That said, eating uncooked mushrooms is not very common and it can lead to gastrointestinal distress. While this is unlikely to lead to serious nausea, a little bit of gas, burping, or a brief wave of nausea isn't uncommon.

You don't have to eat fresh mushrooms on their own; common methods of consumption include eating them with a chocolate bar or dipping them in honey. Chocolate is also known to add a little boost to the mushroom ex-

perience. Putting the mushrooms in a peanut butter sandwich or smoothie are other ways to get them down. However, keep in mind that combining the mushrooms with too much food is likely to work against the potency of the experience.

The experience of consuming fresh versus dehydrated mushrooms will differ in subtle ways, typically, dried mushrooms feeling slightly less potent. In the drying process, P. cubensis mushrooms lose up to about 90 percent of their weight as water; 10 grams of fresh mushrooms are equal in potency to about 1 gram of dried mushrooms. If 3.5 grams of mushrooms are intended to be eaten dried, then the raw equivalent is closer to 35 grams.

Simple Extraction

Hot water or high acidity can be used to extract the psilocybin or predigest some of the mushroom material that would otherwise be broken down by the stomach, thus avoiding the gastrointestinal and flavor challenges of fresh mushrooms. These methods typically yield a faster onset, more intense peak, and shorter overall duration.

Hot Water

If the most common way of using psilocybin—eating the mushrooms—doesn't appeal, you can opt for the second most common way, tea made with fresh or dried mushrooms. People have their own rituals, but at their core is a simple steep. Simply pour boiling water over the desired quantity of chopped or powderized mushroom material and allow the mixture to steep for around 15 minutes or until cool enough to consume.

This method allows for many options, because other varieties of tea or herbs can be added to the mix. Ginger and honey are common mixers for taste and to help settle the stomach. Various additives have their own subtle impact on the journey. Cocoa has a stimulating and opening effect that can further potentiate the experience thanks to its theobromine content.

While the options are varied and limitless, this method need not be complicated. If using chopped mushrooms, you may decide to remove the mushrooms after steeping or you may choose to consume them. If using powdered mushrooms, leaving them in the brew may be easier than trying to remove them.

Making Mushroom Tea

1. Boil water for the tea. If using ginger, add it to the water for about 10 minutes before boiling.
2. Measure out the desired dose of fresh or dried mushrooms.
3. Roughly chop the fresh mushrooms or chop or powderize the dried mushrooms, and place in a mug.
4. When the water has boiled, pour it over the mushrooms. If desired, add a tea bag.
5. Allow 15 minutes to pass before consuming the tea.
6. Optionally strain the mushrooms before consuming.

Acid Extract (Lemon Tek)

This method uses lemon juice, which is extremely acidic, to extract psilocybin and predigest the mushroom body. Simply submerge the desired quantity of ground or powderized dried mushrooms in either freshly squeezed or bottled lemon juice and let it sit for 30 minutes. As with the mushroom tea, completely removing the mushroom material is optional, although any remaining material may have a larger impact because such little liquid is used. The lemon extract itself can be combined with tea or another beverage or taken as a straight shot. The extract has a faster and more intense come up, peak, and come down than either fresh mushrooms eaten on their own or mushroom tea.

Making Lemon Extract

1. Measure out the desired dose of dried mushrooms.

2. Pulverize or powderize the mushrooms, and place in a small bowl or glass.

3. Cover the mushroom material with lemon juice and wait for 30 minutes.

4. Consume the lemon extract as a shot, briefly stirring it before consumption, or mix it into a tea or other beverage so that it goes down more easily.

Microdosing

There is no better place to start the journey into the unknown than with a microdose. The idea of taking tiny doses of psychoactive substances has been a tradition in ancient cultures for longer than we know and reemerged in the 1970s, when psychologist and author James Fadiman coined the term "microdosing." It has taken nearly 40 years for this practice to come into widespread use.

While microdosing may be just a kicking-off point to your exploration of higher doses, it is an effective tool for many people in developing new and improved habits, ceasing addiction, and dealing with depression, symptoms of PMS, and other ailments. Still, it is not a surefire way to fix a problem; rather, your personal exploration will highlight the potential benefits for you.

The most important thing to remember throughout your microdosing journey is that change is the only constant. Get to know the mushroom. Take baby steps in building a relationship, and don't be afraid to push your boundaries—but in a safe way.

Average Dose

Finding the sweet spot is most frequently associated with microdosing, because tiny adjustments in dose can have a significant impact. Although commonly reported as 0.1 gram (100 mg), "microdose" is the term that describes the average dose. That may be the right spot for you, but the effect of a microdose depends just as much on the potency of the mushroom as it does on the dose. Remember, your sweet spot can change with the strain, batch, freshness, and quality of mushrooms being used. This is one of the best reasons to grow your own mushrooms, so you can maintain a consistent and high-quality supply.

Boosting a Microdose

A common mistake for new microdosers occurs when they don't feel what they expected and take a second dose to make up the difference. Often, the result is unnecessary anxiety, canceled plans, and potential danger if it coincides with driving or other activities. Just be patient, allow a day or two to pass, and try again with a slightly larger microdose.

Intended Feel

The official statement on the intended feel of a microdose is that it should be subperceptual. Often, this is taken to mean that you shouldn't feel an effect. However, Fadiman, who also coined the term "subperceptual" in this context, explains: "The flowers and trees should be more vibrant, but they should not be talking to you." You are supposed to notice something, to feel something, but it shouldn't be the feeling that you have ingested a psychedelic substance.

When you're seeking your sweet spot, it is helpful to take days off between use, then slowly increment upward until you reach an upper limit that edges on the not-so-normal or not-so-comfortable. After that, slowly increment back down until you settle on the right dose for you. This is typically done in increments as small as 0.05 gram (50 mg), and some fine-tuning of 0.025 gram (25 mg) increments can further refine the experience, although most people won't notice such small adjustments.

While your sweet spot may not be typical, here are a few touchstones to give you an idea of how varying doses affect most people.

0.05 gram (50 mg). No perceptible effect to the average person. With experience, the effect may be felt, but only slightly. Very mild heightening of the senses.

0.1 gram (100 mg). A slight heightening of the senses, typically perceptible to more sensitive individuals.

0.2 gram (200 mg). A definite heightening of the senses and more than a functional microdose for the average person.

0.3 gram (300 mg). Closer to a threshold dose. Expect to experience an altered state beyond mild enhancement. Feeling some anxiety while trying to function normally at this dose is common.

Microdosing Best Practice

Choose something familiar. When microdosing, it is always best to begin experimenting within the realm of what is familiar to you. This may mean trying a microdose on your favorite hike, while walking your dog, or with your morning coffee on a day off work. The point is to set yourself up with an experience that is normal to you, increasing the chances that you will notice even subtle changes.

Reflect. A variety of reflection-based practices can help you perceive the effects of microdosing. Journaling may be the most helpful because it allows for reflection on past days, building a larger narrative as time goes on. Although one of the more intensive methods of reflection, it is recommended at least for the phase of finding your sweet spot for the first time.

When you begin to microdose, tracking your days on and off is also fruitful. Because the effects tend to be more cumulative than immediate, you may overlook small but significant shifts that occur. By taking a moment to track small changes, you will have a much better idea whether or not this practice was beneficial to you and to what degree.

Use a jewelry scale. Clearly, the quantity of mushroom material needed for a microdose is very small, making it hard to eyeball and almost impossible to do consistently without the right tools. The best tool is a scale that can accurately measure to three decimal points and to a single milligram. You'll find many choices online, often for less than $20.

Powderize 3 to 5 grams at a time. Preparing mushrooms for microdosing is best accomplished by powderizing in a coffee grinder, although using a mortar and pestle or crushing between your fingers will also do the job. Powderizing all your mushrooms at once may seem like a good idea, but it isn't. Stored powderized mushrooms degrade in potency more quickly than whole mushrooms do. It is best to prepare only a month or two of microdoses in advance, typically about 3 to 5 grams.

Store mushroom powder with desiccant. As with all mushroom storage, results are best when the container is at zero percent humidity. Whenever possible, include food-grade silica desiccant pouches with the mushroom powder. Because powderized mushrooms have a higher surface area than whole mushrooms, they are even more susceptible to the damaging effects of humidity and oxidation.

Commit to a schedule and protocol. Taking a microdose as part of a routine is the best way to experience the benefits. Regardless of the protocol you choose (various protocols are shown in this section), make a commitment and stick to it. The commitment period is usually 4 to 6 weeks followed by some time off from dosing, usually at least 2 weeks. Also think about time of day. Choose a time when you're not rushed. If you find that you are among the minority of people who feel deeply tired when taking a microdose, then consider doing it in the evening or even right before bed.

Focus on the day, not the dose. The goal of a microdose is a subtle assist. Don't focus too much on whether you felt the dose, but instead on whether you had a good day. At its best, microdosing leads to improvements that will last throughout the day.

Preparing Microdose Capsules

Although you can take a dose directly by eating it or mixing it into water, a cup of coffee, or your morning oatmeal, preparing your own capsules will save you the time and effort of weighing out the right dose each time. Depending on the model, a capsule-filling machine can easily produce 24 to 100 capsules in just 15 to 45 minutes.

Here are a few tips that go a long way in ensuring consistent dosing. Because most capsule-filling machines have their own instructions, this is just general advice instead of a specific method.

- Decide on the size of capsule machine and capsules to purchase. Size doesn't really matter, although smaller (size 0 or 1) saves money on

Steps to filling your own capsules.

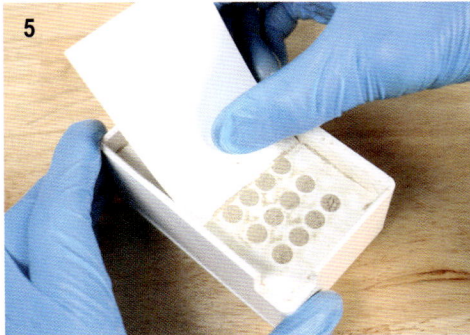

1. Weigh & prep capsule for measurement both with and without supplement.
2. Weigh the required quantity of mushroom and supplement; blend together to an ultra fine consistency.
3. Place capsule caps and bodies in the machine.
4. Pour the first ¼ of powder into the bodies.
5. Use the scraper to pack the bodies.
6. With all powder packed in, squeeze cap down into bodies.
7. Remove ready-to-use capsules.

additional supplements, and larger (size 00 or 000) allows more room for additional beneficial supplements.

- Purchase capsules that are already separated into caps and bodies to save time manually separating them.
- Grind the mushrooms into a powder and mix it with a secondary ingredient to make sure there is enough material to fill each capsule. Any supplement or filler will do the trick as long as it is a fine powder. Lion's mane mushroom is a common choice for its brain-boosting effects. Brown rice flour is a good neutral additive.
- Weigh the ingredients in one test capsule, adding the known quantity of mushroom material, taring the scale, and then finding the necessary quantity of additional supplement before multiplying that number to get the total needed for all the capsules that will be filled. Distribute the powder into the capsules and pack it in as much as possible with a pencil eraser or similar utensil.

Popular Microdose Protocols

In the case of microdosing, a protocol is a schedule of the days of the week that a microdose is taken. It provides structure in a practice that leans heavily into subtle effects. Here are the most common microdose protocols.

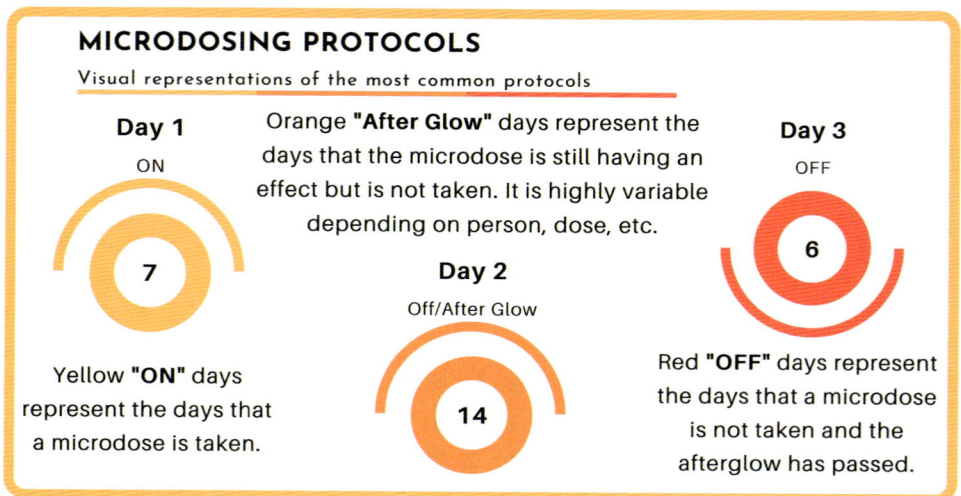

MICRODOSING PROTOCOLS

Visual representations of the most common protocols

Day 1
ON

7

Orange **"After Glow"** days represent the days that the microdose is still having an effect but is not taken. It is highly variable depending on person, dose, etc.

Day 2
Off/After Glow

14

Day 3
OFF

6

Yellow **"ON"** days represent the days that a microdose is taken.

Red **"OFF"** days represent the days that a microdose is not taken and the afterglow has passed.

Fadiman Protocol

This protocol is named for James Fadiman, who coined the term "microdosing." He applied a standard pharmaceutical research protocol to microdosing when he began to explore the concept in the 1970s. The off days are meant to prevent the buildup of tolerance and also aid in the integration process.

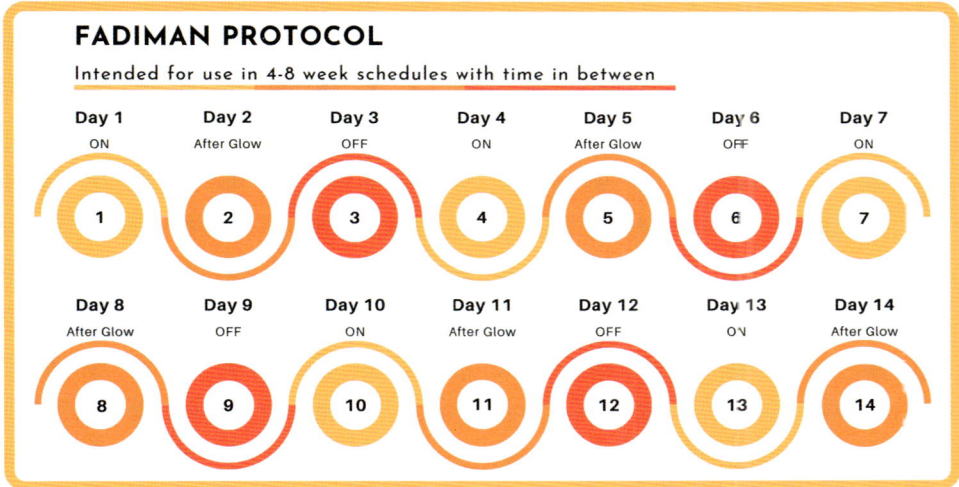

FADIMAN PROTOCOL

Intended for use in 4-8 week schedules with time in between

Day 1	Day 2	Day 3	Day 4	Day 5	Day 6	Day 7
ON	After Glow	OFF	ON	After Glow	OFF	ON
1	2	3	4	5	6	7

Day 8	Day 9	Day 10	Day 11	Day 12	Day 13	Day 14
After Glow	OFF	ON	After Glow	OFF	ON	After Glow
8	9	10	11	12	13	14

Modified Fadiman Protocol

This protocol mimics the intention of the original Fadiman protocol but is adjusted slightly to provide a consistent flow from week to week. Dose days and off days fall on the same days of the week, one week after the other.

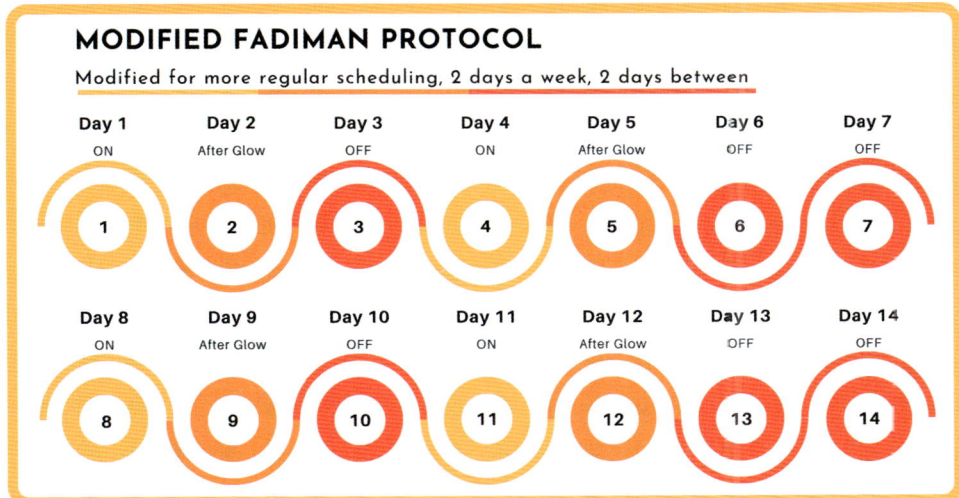

MODIFIED FADIMAN PROTOCOL

Modified for more regular scheduling, 2 days a week, 2 days between

Day 1	Day 2	Day 3	Day 4	Day 5	Day 6	Day 7
ON	After Glow	OFF	ON	After Glow	OFF	OFF
1	2	3	4	5	6	7

Day 8	Day 9	Day 10	Day 11	Day 12	Day 13	Day 14
ON	After Glow	OFF	ON	After Glow	OFF	OFF
8	9	10	11	12	13	14

Stamets Protocol

Named after renowned mycologist Paul Stamets, this protocol is designed to maximize neurogenesis, or new growth of the myelin sheath of the nervous system as well as brain cells. Psilocybin is theorized to stimulate the body's own production of nerve growth factor (NGF), and so is lion's mane mushroom. Vitamin B3 (flushing niacin) is used to open up the capillaries and increase the distribution of active compounds, maximizing the therapeutic benefit of these compounds.

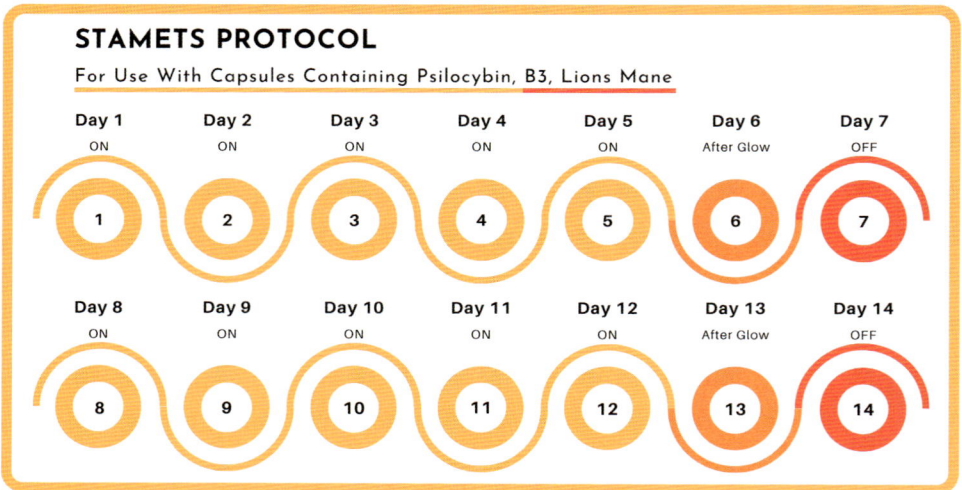

STAMETS PROTOCOL

For Use With Capsules Containing Psilocybin, B3, Lions Mane

Day 1	Day 2	Day 3	Day 4	Day 5	Day 6	Day 7
ON	ON	ON	ON	ON	After Glow	OFF
1	2	3	4	5	6	7

Day 8	Day 9	Day 10	Day 11	Day 12	Day 13	Day 14
ON	ON	ON	ON	ON	After Glow	OFF
8	9	10	11	12	13	14

Caution

When using vitamin B3 (flushing niacin), be careful to dose conservatively. Even doses as small as 0.1 gram (100 mg) can lead to red skin, sweating, and an itching sensation throughout the body for 15 minutes or longer.

Microdosing Institute Protocol

With this protocol, Microdosing Institute, a very active Netherlands-based organization with lots of on-the-ground and some institutional research, normalized an intuitive protocol some of their community users had adopted. There is no direct intention associated with this protocol other than the fact that some people prefer it.

MICRODOSING INSTITUTE PROTOCOL

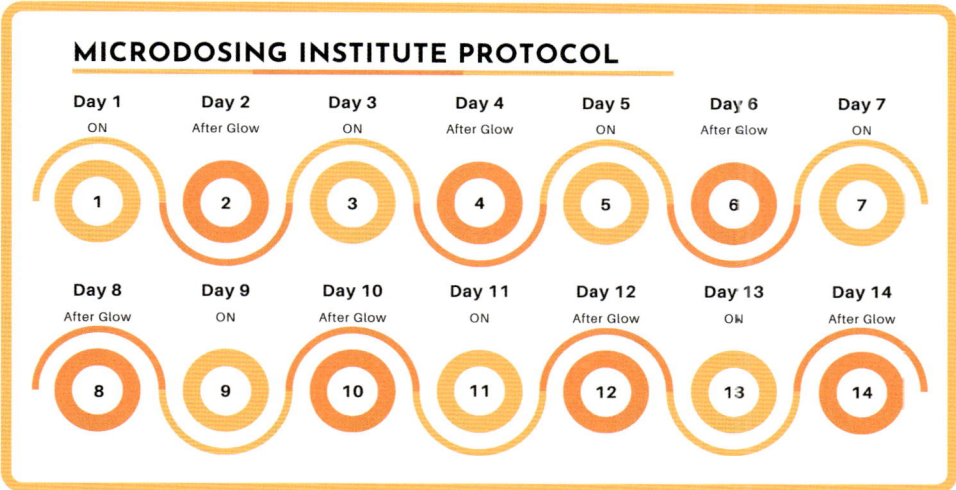

Day 1	Day 2	Day 3	Day 4	Day 5	Day 6	Day 7
ON	After Glow	ON	After Glow	ON	After Glow	ON
1	2	3	4	5	6	7

Day 8	Day 9	Day 10	Day 11	Day 12	Day 13	Day 14
After Glow	ON	After Glow	ON	After Glow	ON	After Glow
8	9	10	11	12	13	14

The Intuitive Protocol

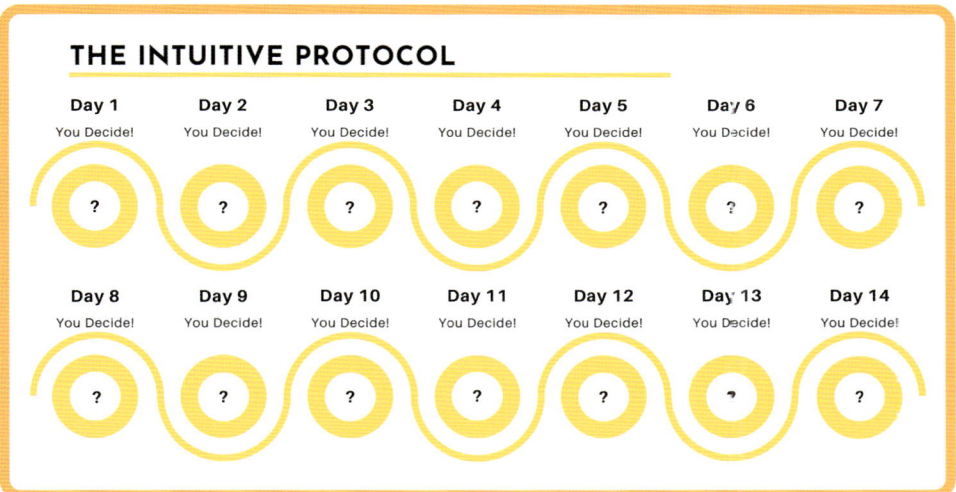

This is not a protocol but a concept. The idea is that, unlike pharmaceuticals, microdosing can help address root causes of issues and eventually be used with less frequency. Many people find that they benefit most from microdosing in response to a particular mental or emotional state and take a microdose in response. Ultimately, you will learn to define your own relationship to microdosing, which does not have to be highly regimented.

THE INTUITIVE PROTOCOL

Day 1	Day 2	Day 3	Day 4	Day 5	Day 6	Day 7
You Decide!	You Decide!	You Decide!	You Decide!	You Decide!	You Decide!	You Decide!
?	?	?	?	?	?	?

Day 8	Day 9	Day 10	Day 11	Day 12	Day 13	Day 14
You Decide!	You Decide!	You Decide!	You Decide!	You Decide!	You Decide!	You Decide!
?	?	?	?	?	?	?

Macrodosing

Unlike microdosing, which produces subtle effects, macrodosing uses larger doses to alter consciousness and often dramatically heighten perception and emotions. Altering consciousness with mushrooms is new for most people, although altering states of consciousness generally is commonplace. The average person will flow through a wide variety of experiences daily, undergoing different energy levels, emotional states, thought processes, and chemically induced shifts. A large dose of psilocybin greatly magnifies these experiences.

While surrendering is essential to make the most of an experience with mushrooms, there are skills that can be developed and actions taken to influence the depth of impact that the experience will have. When working with psilocybin, take it step-by-step, feeling it out at smaller doses before deciding to macrodose.

Move toward the Light, Prepare for the Darkness

Mushrooms unlock doors to our own deeper truths relentlessly. In comparison with other psychedelics, psilocybin seems to have a mind of its own, which makes highly focused and issue-specific work more challenging. Psilocybin creates a roller coaster ride with ups, downs, twists, and turns that may be exhilarating, scary, painful, or suspenseful—or gentle, peaceful, fun, and exciting. You may experience the whole range of these emotions in a single trip.

For many psilocybin users, a positive experience does not necessarily correlate to "felt good." Even a "peak experience" can be construed as euphoric, but just as easily it might be a cathartic release. Catharsis—perhaps reliving past traumas, screaming, shouting, and shaking—can result in tremendous benefit and personal growth.

Experiences on psilocybin are typically not so extreme, but reviewing discomfort or becoming aware of otherwise normalized discomforts is a very common experience. Your reaction to the content determines the trajectory of your experience. For this reason, it is best to decouple "good" from "feels good" and "bad" from "feels uncomfortable." Simply do your best to appreciate the meaning and potential lessons.

You can view psilocybin as an ally sifting through your memory and your habits and helping you to look at things differently. Being prepared for darkness is different from expecting it, but to grow you must eventually leave your comfort zone and face your boundaries . There is no escaping the shadowy darkness that we all carry with us in life. When that material washes up on your shores, the best thing to do is look, listen, and engage with it. This is one of the biggest growth stimuli for most people, simply facing themselves.

It is this inherent dance with darkness, whether within you or around you, that is the ultimate challenge for new journeyers.

Caution

Not every bad trip can be immediately labeled a diamond in the rough. Particularly for individuals who have experienced significant trauma in their lives, psilocybin can bring up old material and even lost memories that are not easily handled with the help of mushrooms alone. That's why working with a therapist or a guide, or both, is a common recommendation in the burgeoning psychedelic space. Whether those resources are accessible or not, it is best to go into a psychedelic experience with as much support as possible, including from friends or family.

Instead of a challenge, what if this were an opportunity to know yourself in a whole new way? This reframe is at the core of the mindset of psilocybin use. Ultimately, some of the mind's most important work is to limit the constant deluge of information and weave together narratives with the information it takes in. The human mind is a meaning-making machine, and the conscious observer can take great strides with a simple understanding that this meaning-making can be a conscious process.

Harm Reduction and Personal Growth

One way of looking at the negative feelings associated with psychedelic use is "having a bad trip." Through a therapeutic lens, there is room to reframe a bad trip into a challenging experience. A bad trip is a dead end, but a difficult experience is the beginning of a new journey, inviting questions such as, Why was that difficult? What was so scary or hurt so much?

Modern psychedelic use is far different from traditional use, which has almost always been held in the intimate context of community, among peers who understand the experience and have long-standing traditions that support the preparation, navigation, and integration of the psychedelic experience. Now that many psilocybin users experiment alone or in the presence of uninformed individuals, some education on set, setting, preparation, navigation, and integration—the five factors that form the blueprint of a holistic psychedelic experience—is helpful. It is up to you to fill in the details and animate the experience with your own effort and intentionality.

Set

Set, short for mindset, is the first half of the iconic phrase "set and setting." It refers to a broad-ranging awareness of your own mind that can be useful in bringing more intention to the experience. It is the awareness that what is in your mind will be magnified, that what is in your mind matters. Cultural and societal programming does a lot to suppress certain aspects of self. We all have these shadowy parts that have a way of making themselves known during a psychedelic experience, and getting to know them can be one of the most healing aspects of mushroom use. On the other hand, if you only want to feel blissed out and heavily resist these shadowy aspects, then the result can be a constricting struggle.

When it comes to mindset and mushrooms, the work comes before and not during the journey. To better understand your mindset, ask yourself questions: Why do I want to take this journey? What do I expect will happen? What am I hoping will happen? What am I afraid will happen? How will I handle the unexpected? Am I choosing to do this work for myself or for others?

State your intention. It can be something simple, such as, "I seek to release tension and open up." It can be a more specific, such as, "I want to better understand the reason for my tobacco addiction." Here are some considerations that can help in setting an intention.

Intention versus expectation. People often come to mushrooms with the medical model in mind. There is a problem in their life and they want a solution, but this is not how mushrooms work. Setting out with a goal like "I want to lose 50 pounds" or "I want to stop being depressed" creates an expectation for what success will be. The most helpful intentions may have a specific goal in mind, but they invite a process of discovery instead of the expectation of attainment or enlightenment. Intentions burdened with conscious or subconscious expectation can easily become obstacles and get in the way of seeing the bigger possibilities that psilocybin offers.

Expand awareness versus drive toward goals. Mushrooms are not required to count calories, call your mother more often, or spend less time on your phone. Mushrooms work more on the "why" of these behaviors, digging deep into the recesses of the mind. Intentions can easily go hand in hand with goals and desired outcomes, but their strength is in weaving meaning from the bigger picture of your life.

Responsibility. Intentions are best set with an attitude of total personal responsibility. Requiring someone else to change or to behave in a certain way is an easy way to block your path of personal growth and exploration.

Setting

While mindset takes you inward, setting includes everything about the external world you experience while dosing. It encompasses environment, nature and the elements, society and people, convenience, and care.

Most people benefit from a controlled or familiar environment. It might be in your home or your favorite spot in the woods. The key is to set yourself up for success. If you are in your home, that means cleaning the space, maybe getting some good mood lighting, and treating the impending journey as a special occasion. The choice of an outdoor space might mean making sure you have the right clothing and gear to get comfortable and embrace the elements. In either case, you might consider little snacks, hot beverages, and other comforts to support you during or immediately after the experience.

Preparation

The lead-up to the experience includes mental and physical cleansing, gathering support, and focusing intention. Here's a timeline that works well for many journeyers.

Month before the Journey

Preparation begins the moment you decide to do a journey, even if you don't have a specific date lined up. This is a great time to start letting thoughts, feelings, and ideas mingle in your mind. It's also a good time to begin mind-focusing and reflective practices to further explore and craft your mindset.

Meditation skills can meet moments of chaos with calm presence and curiosity or a more observational stance.

Breathwork skills can bring the mind and body back into connection, or just the opposite, launching the mind deeper into psychic space using various patterns of breathing and holding breath.

Journaling strengthens the narrative mind, sharpening an awareness of the stories you tell yourself as well as empowering you to weave the narrative of your choosing with the often-fragmented pieces of self that are uncovered.

Yoga and similar body-centric practices, even lifting weights, can build a deeper connection between mind and body, deepening the conscious release of tightness, or pain in the body and allowing feelings of healing, euphoria, or realignment to enter.

These practices and many like them are known for their ability to increase self-awareness. While they often enhance the use of psilocybin, the inverse may also be true. Psilocybin often enhances these practices. This is not to say they need to be combined. Simply having these varying practices in the same orbit of your life is enough for them to play off one another and create synergistic benefits.

Week before the Journey

Now is the time to deepen into the intentions of the journey and prepare the set and setting of the space. This may be just a couple of days beforehand or it could easily extend beyond just a week in advance. Along with cleaning any clutter in your home, consider cleaning any clutter in your mind. Distancing yourself from social media, constant news feeds, or even family drama can be beneficial. Eliminating processed junk foods for even a day or two before the experience can contribute to a deeper experience. Complete any necessary chores and errands so you'll have ample space on the day of the journey and the day after to put yourself back together and begin the process of integration.

Day of the Journey

The most important preparation for the day of the journey is to maintain a relaxed attitude. If you need to clean and prepare more, do it with care, enjoy it if possible, and try not to rush. Here are more helpful pointers.

Don't drink too much water before dosing. Staying hydrated is important, but drinking a lot of water right before consuming mushrooms can reduce stomach acidity and make for a watered-down experience. If you're thirsty, sipping water is fine and acidic beverages with a high vitamin C content can even enhance the potency of an experience.

Don't eat too much (but eat something). Too much food will dilute the experience. While many sources encourage fasting before a journey, that can dramatically increase the potency of the experience while simultaneously intensifying the risk of low-blood-sugar-induced anxiety. When approaching psilocybin for the first time, eat a light meal a couple of hours prior to the journey. For the more experienced, fasting can be a worthy avenue of exploration.

Consider silent darkness. While there is much to say about music, there is just as much value in simple silence—made famous by Terence McKenna's commitment to the heroic dose, which he called "5 dried grams in silent darkness." The primary benefit of silent darkness is that it commands the mind to confront itself, with no outside scaffolding to lean on.

Consider music. For many journeyers, music is a must. Some use music as a vehicle to explore emotional states more deeply with carefully curated playlists mirroring the ascent peak and descent of the psilocybin journey. Others simply find listening to their favorite tunes therapeutic. Avoid music interrupted by ads or music with lyrics, as simple words can easily become fractals of meaning spinning off into ideas, memories, and other mental material.

Psychedelic playlists are abundant and diverse; a quick search for the term "psilocybin journey playlist" on a search engine or digital music service will turn up a long list of results. Some playlists may be timed to coincide with the average psilocybin journey, intensifying with the peak around 90 minutes to 2 hours in and slowly coming down with the expected trajectory over the next 2 to 3 hours. If it is that kind of playlist, skip the shuffle and play it straight through.

Avoid or ease into any drug combination. It is never a good idea to combine drugs with unknown effects or interactions. This caution is extended to any nonprescription substances, including cannabis, caffeine, and alcohol.

Invoke the sacred. For many people in Western culture, mushrooms may represent a step toward a more intentional or spiritual life. In my personal experience, embracing anything spiritual or sacred felt alien, and even though I wanted to explore, I felt guarded. The book Braiding Sweetgrass by Robin Wall Kimmerer helped me, and I highly recommend it to you. The author was raised with the indigenous values of the Potawatomi Nation and later became a Western ecologist. Her experiences in those realms gave her an understanding of both the materialist, reductionist Western worldview as well as its seeming opposite, a holistic view that sees the whole as more than a sum of its parts. The author's words made the idea of the sacred more available to me, and I began to see the benefit of what could be called cultural technologies. Her perspectives on the term "ceremony" brought me into the deep awareness of what I was really missing out on. Not every psilocybin experience needs to be a ceremony but it is good to know that any journey could be.

Embrace the web of connection. One of the most natural and potentially helpful ways to prepare to use psilocybin is to share your thoughts about your upcoming journey with the person or people who will listen to you. Tell them why you want to do it, what you want out of it, your fears, your

Psychology of the Woo

Why do all this extensive work to prepare for the experience? Why connect to other humans, clean your space, set an intention, talk to a tree? Why journal your thoughts and set goals? For starters, it takes more than the right tools to build a sturdy structure. There is a lot of work that must go into the planning and construction. Similarly, the prejourney steps outlined here are tools that will help you discover your best life with the help of mushrooms.

Increasing conscious awareness is at the root of using mushrooms for personal growth. But what about belief? It seems that psychedelics work best in the space that pharmaceuticals consider their downfall, the power of belief, or the placebo effect. As psychedelics magnify the contents of conscious awareness, the benefits imparted have a lot to do with conscious and subconscious beliefs. How well the mushrooms work, the impact they have, and the direction in which they steer your life inevitably are guided largely by the mindset they are amplifying.

dreams. Getting the who, what, when, where, and particularly why of your journey out of your head and in front of a trusted confidant is a good way to explore yourself a little further. Be a little choosey in this process as the individual's ability to withhold judgment, remain curious, and listen will affect how much they can support your exploration.

Another beneficial area of connection is nature. This might mean simply admiring the life at your doorstep or taking a stroll on the land where the journey will take place, perhaps circling the house. Ultimately, this practice can bring a deeper sense of place and contribute to a feeling of being more grounded and safer during a psilocybin journey.

Navigation

The term "psychedelic" comes from the Greek words "psyche," meaning the soul or mind, and "deloun," meaning to manifest, or readily perceived or made apparent. Think of it as mind manifesting, although soul manifesting might be even more appropriate. Psilocybin, in particular, seems to have an incredible knack for making the otherwise unseen or lesser-known aspects of soul and mind very apparent.

Beyond turning up the receiving power of the user's antenna and lowering the filters of the brain, here are some typical effects that can be experienced.

- Altered perception of time.
- Altered perception of the self, sometimes resulting in an ego dissolution or ego death experience.
- Enhanced sensory perception, leading to intensified colors, patterns, and sounds.
- Emotional and mood changes, ranging from euphoria and bliss to introspection and emotional release.
- Emotional and cathartic experiences, where the user may confront and process unresolved emotions or traumas.
- Self-reflection and insights, some quite critical and others more complimentary.
- A felt sense of interconnection and unity underlying all life.
- Mystical experiences, including transcendence or union with the divine.
- Closed-eye visual phenomena from geometric patterns to entity encounters.
- Open-eye visual distortions from tracers on moving objects to intricate overlays on existing objects, such as faces morphing or tapestry patterns moving of their own accord.
- Dramatic swings in body temperature.
- Nausea and or gastrointestinal distress.

Surrender

As psilocybin takes conscious awareness on a tour through the mind, the best thing to do is go with the flow. Relax into the experience and see where it takes your mind. If challenges arise, meet them in the humble spirit of surrender, allowing them to wash over you and to move through you with as much self-compassion and curiosity as possible. If resistance prevails, it can be useful to delve into the "when" and "why" after the experience. Finding resistance is not a reason to crumble, and the journey toward softening into surrender is where you may learn the most about yourself. Surrender also applies to positive feelings; just be a beach and let them wash over you.

Because of the potential for abuse in the world of psychedelics, keep in mind that surrender applies to the internal experience. If anyone attempts to convince you to surrender to unwanted advances, resistance is the necessary reaction.

Take Notes

Because the psilocybin experience is often dreamlike, taking notes throughout the journey can be hugely beneficial for the integration process. Having notes will make recall of and reflection on the experience much easier. Scribbling in a notepad is likely the least useful option, as writing can conflict with the easy flow of thought and experience. Having a sitter or guide record your spoken thoughts can be a much better means of note taking, but perhaps the most accessible and useful method of recording notes is with a voice recording app.

Recording every moment of the experience isn't necessary and is more likely to get in the way than act as an aid. Try leaving a breadcrumb trail of simple words or phrases unless it feels right to speak your process aloud.

Navigation Timeline

The main journey typically takes place over a period of 4 to 6 hours. It consists of three parts: onset (20 to 45 minutes), peak (1 to 2 hours), and coming down (1½ to 3 hours). After the peak of the experience, there is a gentle return to a relatively normal state of waking consciousness.

The post-journey occurs over about 4 to 12 hours. Once you return to normal consciousness, you should expect to spend some time in energetic recovery. This recovery can include slight nausea, dizziness, and tiredness. Increased appetite is also quite common, so having light snacks on hand is a great idea. Most people feel pretty much back to normal 6 to 8 hours after ingesting mushrooms, but not everyone. You may have a mild hangover, so allow time for full recovery before operating a vehicle or going back to work. A good night's rest is usually enough to feel fully normal.

Integration

This is the time to focus first on resting your body and mind, and then on bringing new downloads and realizations into your everyday life. A long-time essential aspect of the psychedelic experience, integration has only recently been adopted by new and recreational users. The popularity of integration in today's world of psychedelics is one of the differences between using substances primarily for fun and using them more for personal growth.

"Integration" may seem like an abstract term until you substitute "disintegration" for "navigation." Defined as a loss of unity or integrity or breaking into parts, "disintegration" accurately describes the roller coaster ride through amplified aspects of self up to and beyond the perceived loss of identity or ego. While simply coming down from the psychedelic experience allows the self to integrate, or become whole, the integration process offers the opportunity to look over, sort through, and rearrange the many pieces of yourself. The following steps can help you integrate your transformative experience and harness its potential for growth.

Share your journey. Communicate the details of your experience, regardless of its intensity or outcome. Even seemingly minor experiences can lead to valuable insights and personal development. Journaling for yourself and discussing your story with supportive friends or family members can help you continue the process of reflection and solidify the healing potential within your psyche. Remember, the meaning of your experience is often shaped by your interpretation and understanding.

Reflect on your original intentions. Revisit the initial goals or intentions you set before embarking on your journey. Even if the experience seems unrelated at first, dedicate some time to explore the connection. The significance of your experience may become clearer as you contemplate it in light of your original intentions.

Identify themes of transformative experience. To delve deeper into your experiences, think about how your journey affected you physically, mentally, emotionally, and spiritually. Consider whether you feel that your levels of confidence and self-esteem grew, and whether you gained insight into your life purpose and direction.

Seek professional guidance. If you find it difficult to process or integrate your experience on your own, consider seeking the help of a professional therapist, counselor, or coach. Professionals trained in working with altered states of consciousness and personal growth can provide valuable insights, support, and guidance. While professional support is not a necessity for everyone, working with trained professionals can be beneficial for anyone.

Implementing Transformations

Profound experiences, perspective-altering realizations, and moments of divine connection can be incredibly powerful. However, for a psilocybin journey to have a lasting impact on your life, you must take action and make adjustments. While some small changes may occur naturally, it's crucial to recognize, validate, and nurture these seeds of transformation. Other adjustments might seem challenging, even if they are simple in nature, such as offering an apology or remembering to contact a loved one. Remember, there's no one-size-fits-all advice here—your journey is unique, and the lessons you learn will be too.

It's easier to implement changes immediately after an experience; they become increasingly difficult to maintain upon return to your everyday life.

Additionally, challenges that were once tolerable may become overwhelming. Avoid making reactive decisions or taking drastic actions out of fear. Instead, focus on sustainable growth through small, incremental steps outside your comfort zone. Consistency and gradual progress are the keys to lasting change. If drastic changes are necessary, it's vital to wait at least a week before committing to any major life-altering choice, such as marriage, divorce, or quitting a job.

Keep in mind that only your inner wisdom can guide you on your path. Even though each journey is unique, the following suggestions apply to many experiences:

- Nurture changes that occur naturally and effortlessly.
- Ensure that any changes you make are intentional and practical.
- Reflect on the lessons you've learned before revisiting psilocybin.
- Allow new habits to adapt over time, finding the right balance for sustainability.

Integration Timeline

Day 1: Rest and relaxation. For the hours and day after the experience, a focus on personal restoration is very helpful. This might include a lot of sleep, a walk in the woods, nourishing foods, and other restorative practices.

Days 1 to 3: Afterglow. This is the time to initiate a larger process of reflection on your psilocybin experience. While a longer timeline is fine, stay aware of the highly ephemeral nature of the experience. Now is when you may have a better outlook on life and feel that a "better life" is within your grasp. Know that this is just a phase. By all means, enjoy it but know that holding onto that feeling indefinitely is not possible. Honor this phase and respect the mushroom and yourself by capturing the energy of the afterglow and transforming it into baby steps that will lead you to a better version of yourself.

1 to 2 weeks: Return to normal and do the work. At some point the glow will fade. It is in the absence of psilocybin's optimistic momentum that the real work begins. This is where new rhythms of self-care and balancing come into play. You may find a greater sensitivity to life's challenges. Use your heightened awareness as an opportunity to meet the challenges and make adjustments to your perspective, choice of surroundings, actions, and so on.

1 month: New normal. After the glow has faded, your homework is in progress, and you are pursuing new patterns, it is a good time to check in and see what has changed and what is sticking since the journey. Have any of your original intentions come to fruition?

Beyond. Hopefully, the mushrooms have helped and the journey has opened new aspects of conscious awareness. There is no one way to grow with the ally of psilocybin; it is here to awaken the guide within you. Be sure to emphasize your inner guide, as it is easy to put the power of healing outside yourself. At its best, psilocybin stimulates the healer within you, not to make you return to psilocybin, but to help you return to yourself. Resist the instinct to project this healing intent onto those around you. Instead, cultivate the gift of a healthier you. Doing the work for yourself is always the hardest, but it provides the greatest return on investment and is actually within your control.

A close-up of the gills of a *P. cubensis* fruitbody. Photo by L.G Nicholas

The Mushroom Life Cycle

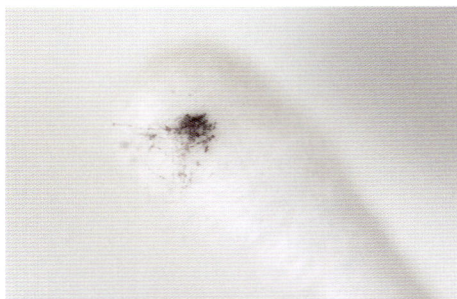

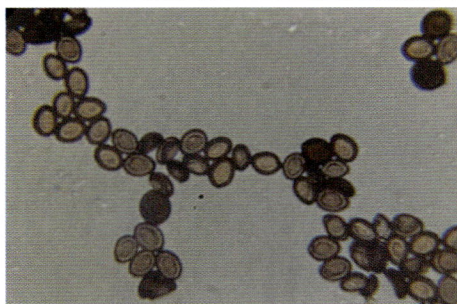

Spores

If mushrooms can grow in the middle of a field in the rain, from a pile of cow dung, how come it takes so much work to get them to grow at home? The idea that it doesn't take much effort in nature is a bit misleading. Nature puts in the work in ways that human cultivators never could. A single mushroom produces millions of spores, reproductive cells borne on the underside of the cap. In nature, the spores are caught by the wind and blown around the environment, where they wait for the ideal growing conditions. A wild mushroom relies on a massive volume of spores and an extremely low likelihood of success; as a cultivator you will rely on an extremely low number of spores and the hope for a high likelihood of success.

The spores of most mushrooms, including psilocybin mushrooms, are haploid, meaning they cannot reproduce without mating. A spore needs to meet another spore during the process of germination, which typically takes 3 to 5 days and can loosely be compared to a plant seed germinating.

Top: The gills of the mushroom contain the spore producing structure known as basidium. Their fan like shape drops the microscopic spores down from the towering mushroom into the air currents below.

Middle: A quick swipe across a spore print can pick up thousands of spores, only visible to the naked eye when clumped together.

Bottom: Under the microscope these otherwise invisible packets of genetic potential begin to stand out. (Photo Credit: Inoculate The World)

Hyphae and Mycelium

When germinating spores bump into other germinating spores, the process is marked by the production of a threadlike structure. This network of filaments, or hyphae, is known collectively as mycelium. Once hyphae connect and begin their more explosive mycelial growth phase, they send out hyphal threads into every direction, expanding in three dimensions.

Ultimately, the job of mycelium is to grow, to seek out suitable living conditions, to digest viable sources of energy, and to invest as much of that energy as possible into passing on its genetics. While different types of mushrooms produce mycelium with varying habits and life cycles, Psilocybe cubensis and similar mushrooms used for home cultivation follow

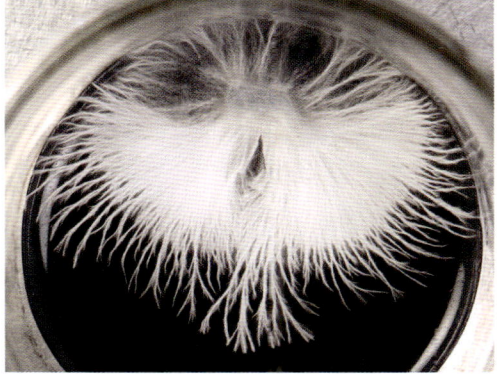

This mycelium growing across a petri dish gives a good look at rhizomorphic mycelial growth. However it doesn't have to look this way in order to produce happy mushrooms.

a single path from spore to fruit (the mushroom) and ultimately exhaust the limited resources provided before becoming mushroom compost. This process is known as colonization. At the point, when the mycelium begins to fully colonize its substrate (the material on which it is growing) and can no longer easily grow, its focus turns toward preparing to fruit.

Primordia and Pins

Once the mycelium has fully colonized its substrate, it begins to produce reproductive organs, mushrooms. The first phase of growth is typically referred to as primordia, which then develop into and become recognizable as pins. This process begins with incredibly small dots of mycelium called hyphal knots. Under the surface, individual hyphal strands weave together to form the birth point of mushrooms.

Pinning is the initial emergence of the mushroom. Once the primordia mature slightly and begin to take the shape of tiny mushrooms, they are referred to as pins. In some cases, these little pins show up here and there, and, in other cases, they cover nearly the entire surface; most typically they are somewhat evenly distributed across the surface of the mycelium.

Often, when there are lots of these little pins, only some of them will graduate to fully mature mushrooms. If there are just a few pins, it is more likely that most or all of them will become mushrooms.

Here we can see the emergence of primordia, small white dots, pins, the slightly more mature mycelial blobs, and even very small mushrooms beginning to take shape.

Maturation

Depending on spore variety, temperature, humidity, fresh air exchange, and other factors, the time between pinning and full maturation can be as quick as 3 to 5 days or as long as 7 to 10 days, or sometimes even longer. However, 3 to 10 days is a reasonable expectation.

Maturation is a gradual process where the cap slowly lifts as the stalk or stipe of the mushroom extends. Sporulation begins after the veil stretches and breaks open, revealing the gills.

Paying close attention to the mushroom's growth at this time really pays off. It's easy to let the mushrooms grow beyond the prime range of maturity in as little as a day. When the pins begin to mature, the mushroom begins with a two-tone distinction on the pin. You can expect this mycelial mass to double in size every day. Increasingly, the cap and stem become distinct aspects of the mushroom, with

These photos follow one tubs maturation progression over 7 days

the stem elongating and the cap looking like an inflating ball at the end of that stick.

As the mushroom nears full maturation, the white margin that connects the cap and stem begins to pull away and the ball-like shape becomes more saucerlike. This is typically the time to harvest the mushroom, before the margin between stem and cap begins to break. As the connecting tissues, or veil, breaks, the edges of the cap quickly unfurl and the spores begin to drop from the gills under the cap.

Sporulation

When the mycelium runs out of space to grow, it switches from colonization to fruiting. While sporulation (the formation of spores) is a beautiful process, essential for the continuation of genetic potential, it is generally considered problematic for the average cultivator.

The problem is that, if you allow spores to drop, they will begin to cover the mushrooms and the inside of the tub. The mushrooms will also typi-

When the gills are fully exposed, expect to see spores falling on all surfaces beneath them.

cally grow larger, but that is only water weight. Unless you are preparing to do more advanced work not covered in this book, like making your own spore syringes, it is best to avoid sporulation by harvesting the mushrooms.

The Cultivation Life Cycle

Starter Culture: Spores or Liquid Culture

Beginners typically use either a spore syringe or a liquid culture syringe to kick off mycelial growth. Ultimately, all mycelium begins with a spore, but this does not mean that every cultivation project uses a spore starter. Liquid culture is the simpler and more foolproof mycelial starting point. Its primary benefit is the ease of expansion and propagation; its downside is the ease with which contaminants can slip through. However, either type of syringe—spore or liquid culture—is a good choice, as long as it's from a reputable supplier.

Spore Syringe

A spore syringe contains 10 to 12 cc/ml of sterile water with spores floating in it. The required quantity of spores is relatively small, and the appearance of the water can vary from almost clear with some small specks of black to nearly black. Because it takes only a few of these microscopic spores to succeed, don't be discouraged by a sparsely filled syringe; typically, it will perform just as well as a fuller syringe. Historically, spore syringes were prone to contamination, but as mycology practices continue to improve, obtaining a totally clean spore syringe is far more common nowadays.

Spores have two important characteristics to consider: they require a few days to germinate before producing mycelium, and they produce inconsistent results. However, they have been the starting point for new growers for a couple of decades.

On the legal side, spore syringes are widely available because they do not contain any psilocybin. Despite having the potential to produce psilocybin in their mycelial phase of growth, the majority of psilocybin-related laws simply outlaw the substance itself; therefore, the spores get a free pass in most locales. However, spore syringes are banned in Idaho and Georgia. Until recently, they were considered banned in California due to strict agricultural policy, but more and more vendors have been shipping them to California with no adverse experiences. It is assumed that the California law is out of date or simply unenforced.

Liquid Culture Syringe

Syringes containing spores share center stage with syringes containing liquid culture. While spore syringes contain spores in sterile water, liquid culture syringes contain the same amount (10 to 12 cc/ml) of nutrient broth and mycelium. The culture is typically cloudlike in appearance, with hyphal threads distributed throughout the syringe.

Until recently, these cultures have been strictly a product of home growers and the underground market because of the understanding that they contain mycelium, which contains psilocybin, and are therefore illegal. With advancements in testing technologies, there is increasing evidence that many strains of fungi produce undetectable levels of psilocybin in the liquid culture state. Among the courageous vendors bucking the system are those working with testing labs who have begun selling syringes of liquid culture that do not test positive for psilocybin. The question remains, What is the legal status of liquid culture? The answer will come in time.

Advantages of Liquid Culture over Spore Syringe

- Significantly faster growth
- More consistent mushroom production
- More mushrooms
- cleaner starting point and lower risk of contamination

While the shift to liquid culture is a big deal in the psilocybin market, in fact, liquid culture has been the standard in traditional culinary and medicinal mushrooms for a long time. The preference for spores over liquid culture is only due to their legality. The benefits of liquid culture are plain: they are created using top-shelf sterile techniques, their genetics have been more highly refined for optimal growth characteristics, and they have a head start because they already contain mycelium.

Spawn

Once you know what your starter culture will be, your goal is to expand it. The go-to method is to inject your culture into sterile grain. The method in this book calls for using ordinary bags of precooked brown rice from a grocery store.

In the world of mushroom cultivation spawn can be created on nearly any type of grain and beyond. This photo shows the use of precooked rice as spawn in its own bag.

When a starter culture is placed on grain, the mycelium begins to expand and consume all the grain in a process known as myceliation, or colonization. Grain is used in this process because it is high in nutrients and sugars, holds moisture well, and has a distinct structure with air gaps to accommodate the mycelium. This environment produces an ideal habitat for mycelium to grow very quickly. And, in using precooked rice, you skip not only the cooking but also the drying, jarring, jar lid preparation, sterilizing, and other laborious steps in producing your own spawn.

Once the starter culture has grown throughout the grain, there is little to see besides glistening white mycelium. This is when it is ready to move to the next phase of the process: bulk substrate.

Bulk Substrate

Compared with spawn, bulk substrate is far less nutritious, is used in higher quantities, and serves more for hydration and structure than as a food source. Many mushrooms are grown on hardwood sawdust or straw. *Psi-*

locybe cubensis mushrooms are often referred to as dung lovers, but they can be grown effectively on a variety of other substrates, including coconut coir alone or the classic CVG, a blend of coconut coir, vermiculite, and gypsum. Growing on nutritious substrates, such as a manure blend, can have some

This project combines the most convenient spawn with the simplest bulk substrate, coconut coir, for maximum ease of use

benefit to your harvest or potentially the potency, but the risk of contamination is greater.

Bulk substrates are combined with spawn at varying ratios, typically between one part spawn to one part bulk and one part spawn to four parts bulk (that is, between 1:1 and 1:4). The more nutritious the bulk substrate, the less additional nutrition is needed from the grain. That means that simpler bulk substrates like coconut coir can produce similar results by increasing the ratio of spawn to substrate. You combine the substrate and spawn in a tub and let the mixture (from this point onward, referred to as "cake") sit until fruiting occurs.

Fruiting

Think of mushrooms in the way you might think of apples. Mushrooms are the fruit of mycelium in much the same way that apples are the fruit of an apple tree. For that reason, it is very common in the world of mushrooms to refer to mushrooms as fruit bodies or fruit, or to call the process of mushrooms growing from the substrate as fruiting.

Keeping It Clean

You may have heard that growing mushrooms is hard because of the potential for contamination. This is a correct statement and an essential understanding for your progress through this book. While clean technique is critical to your success, this entire book is built around simple processes that make a clean workflow as simple as possible. You don't need a laboratory and you don't need to be a scientist to keep your first mycology projects successfully on track and free of contamination.

For clean cultivation, concentrate on four areas: your environment; you, the cultivator; your work materials; and your starter culture.

Checklist

- ❑ Identify and prepare your best potential workspace.
- ❑ Still the air in your workspace for at least 15 minutes.
- ❑ Make sure you and your clothing are clean.
- ❑ Tie back long hair.
- ❑ Remove or tuck away jewelry and accessories.
- ❑ Wear latex gloves and a mask.
- ❑ Clean your hands with 70 percent isopropyl alcohol (ISO).
- ❑ Disinfect your work surface and your work materials with ISO.
- ❑ Make sure all your materials are easily at hand.
- ❑ Move mindfully to prevent excess air movement.
- ❑ Get a starter culture from a trusted source.

Your Environment

Where will you grow your mushrooms? You might do it in your bedroom, walk-in closet, bathroom, kitchen or you might use a combination of spaces—perhaps you'll work on cultivation projects in the bathroom but incubate and fruit the mycelium in a closet. Consider the surfaces you will be working on; they should be easy to clean and to disinfect frequently.

Back patio. No, don't work outdoors. The back patio is only on this list to illustrate what to stay away from. It takes just a slight breeze to blow in some wild spores and ruin your work. You never want to leave colonizing mycelium outside, where the conditions are unpredictable. When using the method of mushroom growing outlined in this book, always work indoors, away from moving fresh air.

Bedroom. A bedroom may seem like a fine place to work. Bedrooms can be totally shut off. The main issue is that they are often full of materials that make great dust magnets including bedding, carpet, curtains, and clothes. Windows or doors may be open on nice days. In most circumstances this is not the best place to work on the project.

Walk-in closet. Like a bedroom, a closet may be full of fabrics and other items that can collect potential contaminants. However, an orderly closed closet typically has very little air movement and is a smaller and easier environment to control. A closet is a good choice for both working on the project and incubation and fruiting.

Kitchen. This part of the home has pros and cons The kitchen counter might make a great and easy-to-disinfect work surface. The downside is the risk of high traffic. Your kitchen might be a good choice.

Bathroom. A bathroom equipped with a shower is a great place to start your mycology project as long as it has a countertop, even if makeshift, to work on. It offers multiple benefits because it is a small private space, is easy to get still air, and is easy to clean and disinfect.

The shower provides an opportunity to clean yourself before starting the project. Just as important, the water vapor in the air from the shower

Extra Clean: Bathroom Tek

Some situations may require more than a room with still air. Pet dander and other allergens float in the air and increase the risk of contamination. Bathroom tek has saved millions of projects. All it takes is a bathroom equipped with a shower and a workspace.

- Remove towels and carpets, dust all surfaces, and sweep or vacuum the floor.
- Still the air. If you have an exhaust fan that turns on with the light, cover it with a lightweight plastic bag or something similar.
- The shower is a multipurpose ally. Turn on the hot water and steam up the whole bathroom.
- When the steam has become dense and foggy, filling the space, lower the water temperature and take a quick shower.
- The water vapor particles capture the contaminating dust particles in the air. When the air cools, the vapor will settle along with the particles and contaminants. With little effort, you fully cleansed the air in your bathroom!
- Wear freshly laundered clothing.
- Wear a surgical mask and hygienic gloves.
- Wipe down surfaces and tools with 70 percent ISO.
- Get to work!

captures solid particles. Don't turn the vent on. If it's regulated by the same switch as the light, cover it with a plastic bag to prevent any air flow.

Using the bathroom, shower, and water vapor combination has long been referred to as bathroom tek. It is very effective. This level of cleanliness is overkill for the techniques described in this book. However, the cleaner option is the better option.

Work Surface

Make sure your workspace has a clean work surface. Finished surfaces, such as sealed wood, granite, plastic, and tile, are fine. Avoid anything absorbent such as cloth or unfinished wood; they're hard to disinfect properly. If you are having trouble finding a good surface, you can always tape a clean trash bag or other plastic film to the surface. Before beginning your work, always disinfect the work surface by spraying it with 70 percent isopropyl alcohol (ISO).

Spruce Up Your Space

You can improve your workspace by cleaning:

- Remove unnecessary clutter.
- weep or vacuum the floor.
- Remove fabric.
- Run an air filter in your home or workspace.
- Maintain still air for at least 15 minutes prior to working in the space.

Still Air

Still air is a constant consideration, because air is the medium through which contaminants find their way into a project. Just as debris naturally settles to the bottom of a glass of muddy water, contaminants settle over time. Air movement lifts and sends dust and other contaminants flying around. Time in stillness allows it to settle. Allow at least 15 minutes of completely still air before beginning to work on a mycology project. Close windows and closing or turning off ventilation and fans.

Still air box. If your environment is particularly dirty or difficult to work in, you might might want to use a still air box. The concept is simple: a simple clear storage bin works as a secondary buffer against any potential air movement. Historically, this method has been understood as something that has to be made, typically by melting or cutting circular armholes in the side of the tub. Fortunately, an unmodified still air box takes less effort and works just as well.

To use an unmodified still air box:

- Get a clear plastic storage bin, around 56 quarts or larger.
- Remove the lid, and disinfect the inside of the bin with 70 percent ISO.
- Place the bin upside down on a disinfected work surface. There is typically a long side and a short side of the tub, and you can choose

which works best for you, with the awareness that the short side will keep a little less air flowing through and improve the overall cleanliness a bit.

- Move the bin so that it hangs over the edge of your work surface with enough gap (about 6 inches) to place your arms inside and move them around comfortably.
- Place a piece of masking or other sturdy, nonmarking tape to the back edge to secure the tub in place and create a small hinge, if you need to lift the tub for any reason.
- You will need to use the box only in the first part of the project, when adding starter culture to the rice bags. After that, you may still choose to use it, but it's far less important.

You, the Cultivator

Now it's time to talk about you. You are dirty. It's not a matter of how much you bathe; it's just a fact of life, the little bits of dust and spores that travel through the air mean that every breath you take contains some amount of environmental contaminants. For most humans, this isn't an issue, because we have the immune system to fight it off, but that is not the case with the extremely vulnerable rice that the mycelium grows on. The following are most important during the first phase of cultivation but still should be observed throughout the various phases.

Face mask. As a cultivator, you want to do your best to still the air from your breath. A cloth, surgical, or N95 mask is best.

Movement. Consider how you move through a space. You can undo the good work of waiting 15 minutes to still the air by excitedly opening a door and blasting an air wave through the room. Instead, open the door slowly and gently, but preferably not at all. Better, have all your materials in the room, close the door, and then do your prep. You can improve your success by moving mindfully through the space and having all your materials at hand.

Body and clothing. Be conscious of what your body and clothing might bring into the space. Showering and putting on clean clothes before starting to work are pluses. If you decide on bathroom tek, consider it a clothing optional method.

Hair. If you have long hair, simply tie it back and out of the way..

Jewelry and accessories. Wear disposable gloves or washable rubber gloves. To avoid them tearing, remove any protruding rings. Bracelets that can be tucked into the gloves are okay, but otherwise remove anything from your wrists.

Hands. If, for some reason, you cannot use disposable gloves, be sure to deep clean your hands prior to working; including your wrists and forearms is wise. It's important to spray your hands (gloved or not) and working materials frequently with 70 percent ISO. If you opt out of wearing gloves, your hands will sting should you have any cuts or scrapes.

A quick procedure for deep cleaning your hands with ISO from a spray bottle goes like this:

- Spray 2 or 3 squirts into the palm of one hand.
- Put your hands together and rub the alcohol across your palms, the backs of your hands, and between your fingers. You want full coverage.
- Spray 2 or 3 squirts into the palm of one hand and clean the opposite wrist and forearm.
- Repeat for the other wrist and forearm.
- Allow a moment for the alcohol to evaporate before beginning your project.

Your Materials

At this point, it's no mystery that 70 percent ISO will be a constant companion in the world of mushroom cultivation. It is your best defense against environmental contaminants as it quickly and effectively disinfects surfaces, and deeply penetrates the cell walls and membranes of organisms. Upon evaporation, the alcohol essentially turns the organism inside out, killing it or at least rendering it unviable. The magic of 70 percent ISO is actually in the 30 percent that is water. This particular ratio has the greatest ability to penetrate deeply into the organism before quickly evaporating, so use it and not 90 percent ISO or 50 percent ISO.

The best way to apply ISO, so that it covers entire surfaces, is with a spray bottle and a paper towel. You could use a spray bottle on its own, but an alcohol-soaked paper towel helps spread the sprayed alcohol across the surface.

Needles. Starter cultures will arrive in a sterile syringe with a sterile needle. Once you start using the needle, you'll have to sterilize it fairly often. While some people may have success using only 70 percent ISO to clean needles, sterilization with an open flame is the standard. See Flame-Sterilizing the Syringe Needle in the Phase 2 procedures section.

Coconut coir. There is no need to clean coconut coir (the substrate that comes into play in Phase 2 of the project) with alcohol. Coconut coir is very resistant to contamination, especially when purchased as a compressed block, which has been heat pressed in a way that enhances cleanliness. Once hydrated with boiling water, coconut coir can be considered sterile enough for a project

Your Starter Culture

Cleanliness is most essential in your starter culture, although the starter is easy to overlook as a potential issue. While you have little control over the cleanliness of starter culture ordered online, the one thing you can do is to purchase from a trusted source. For more information on spore syringes and liquid culture syringes, the easiest starting point for beginners, see The Cultivation Life Cycle and Starter Culture in the Phase 1 materials section.

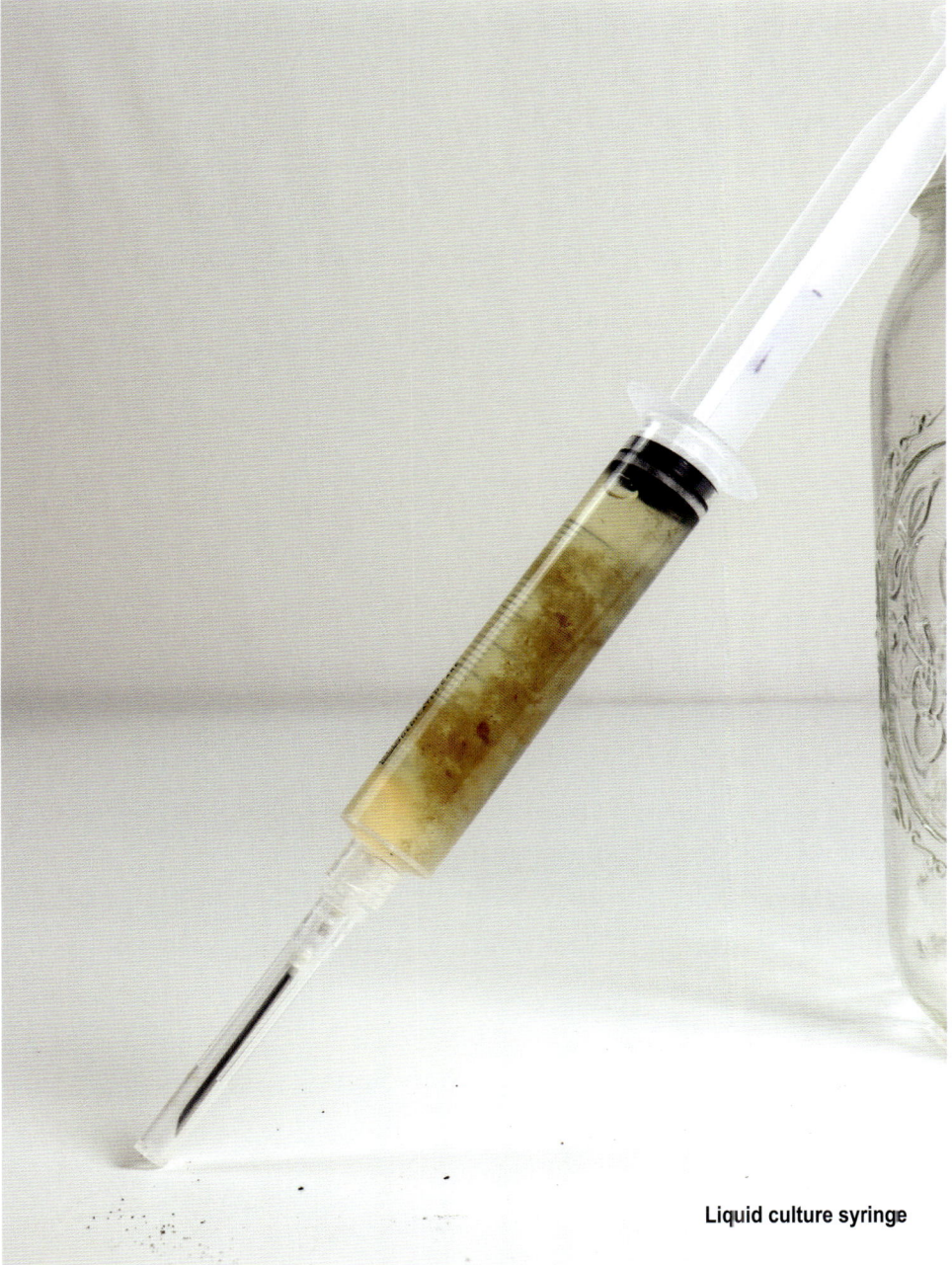

Liquid culture syringe

Ready, Set, Grow!

The method described in this book can't be credited to any one person; it's a culmination of many people in the mushroom cultivation community making small additions and refinements. The most descriptive name for this core technique is the Unmodified Precooked Rice Bag Shoebox. More common names are Unmodified Ready Rice Shoebox, Uncle Ben's Tek and Unmodified Shoebox Tek. These are all suitable search terms to learn more about on the internet.

Let's break down the name Unmodified Precooked Rice Bag Shoebox into its three components:

Unmodified means no modifications are made to the plastic tub used for growing the mushrooms.

Precooked rice bag describes a wide variety of products that are essentially single-serving packets of precooked brown rice normally heated in the microwave before eating—although you won't be warming them. By using precooked rice bags, you are able to skip the steps of preparing the grain and sterilizing it that are typically necessary for mycology projects.
Shoebox refers to the size of the plastic tub being used, typically 6 quarts. Although larger sizes up to 16 quarts work well, it is best to start small.

This simple growing method consists of three phases, each with several tasks:

Phase 1: Colonizing Precooked Rice Bags
- ❑ Create air exchange vents.
- ❑ Break up the tightly packed rice.
- ❑ Inject the starter culture.

❑ Give the bags warmth and still air for 2 to 4 weeks during the colonization process.

Phase 2: Expanding Rice Bags to Shoeboxes
❑ Weigh and break up the coconut coir.
❑ Pour boiling water over the coconut coir.
❑ Break up the colonized rice.
❑ Combine the colonized rice with the cooled coconut coir.
❑ Give the tub warmth and still air for 2 to 4 weeks during the colonization and fruiting process.

Phase 3: Harvest, Storage, and Continued Maintenance
❑ Select mature mushrooms and pick them.
❑ Dehydrate the harvested mushrooms until cracker dry.
❑ Store the dried mushrooms properly for long-term preservation.
❑ Clean the cake after harvest.

General Timeline
- Inoculation and colonization of the rice bags

    Liquid culture: about 2 weeks

    Spore syringe: about 3 weeks
- Spawning to coconut coir, myceliation, and pinning: about 3 weeks
- Maturation and fruiting: about 1 week
- Total time of growth

    Liquid culture syringe: about 5 to 6 weeks

    Spore syringe: about 7 to 8 weeks

Phase 1: Colonizing Precooked Rice Bags

Materials

Online

This book suggests the types of stores where you can purchase the materials required for each of the three phases of cultivation. Online isn't listed, because basically everything is available online now!

Checklist

- ❑ Precooked bags of brown rice
- ❑ Paper surgical tape or filter stickers
- ❑ 70 percent isopropyl alcohol (ISO)
- ❑ Spray bottle
- ❑ Paper towels
- ❑ Lighter
- ❑ Starter culture (spore syringes or liquid culture syringes)
- ❑ Permanent marker
- ❑ Clear tub, 56 quarts or larger, for still air box (optional)
- ❑ Space heater (optional)
- ❑ Large container or plastic tubs and aquarium heater for incubation (optional)

Precooked Bags of Brown Rice

Where to purchase

Grocery Store

What is it?

A precooked bag of brown rice is an amazing tool that mimics a ready-made

bag of sterile grain sold online for mycology purposes. The brand of rice you choose isn't important—just make sure the rice is fully cooked (a package typically calls for a 90-second heating time); it's brown rice, meaning that it's whole grain; and there are no flavoring or seasonings added (but it's normal for a small amount of oil to be included).

Many bags have a clear bottom, which makes viewing the colonization, or growth of mycelium, very straightforward and removes a lot of guesswork. This viewing window is not always available, nor is it essential, but it is helpful, especially for new cultivators.

Why use it?

The reason is simplicity. Before this convenience product was available, it was the grower's responsibility to prepare and sterilize grain. Well-hydrated sterile grain is essential to the mycology process. It is used to create spawn, or the nutrition source for mushroom development, because it provides a sugar- and nutrient-rich food source for fungi, absorbs enough water to keep the mycelium healthy and growing fast, and has many tiny air channels between the grains that allow the mycelium to spread quickly.

Pro Tip

Use two bags of rice per tub. Although a single bag technically is enough, it generally won't produce a good flush of mushrooms. For first timers, it is best to prepare an extra bag beyond what you need in case anything goes wrong.

Paper Surgical Tape or Filter Stickers

Where to purchase
Pharmacy for tape or microppose. com for filter stickers

What is it?
Micropore, or paper surgical tape is tape with microscopic holes across the entire surface. It is typically available at pharmacies as its primary use is in first aid. Paying a little extra for a version of the tape that comes with a dispenser is worthwhile to prevent the tape from sticking to your gloves while applying it.

Instead of tape, you can opt for premade filter stickers from the company Microppose. Be aware that knock-off versions available from some other internet sellers do not perform the same function as they are nonporous and essentially block airflow.

Why use it?

You will be using paper surgical tape or filter stickers to create an air filter for the rice bag. The filter lets a small amount of fresh air in and stale carbon dioxide out of the rice bag while filtering out any hitchhiking spores or bacteria that might contaminate the bag. .

70 Percent Isopropyl Alcohol (ISO, Rubbing Alcohol)

Where to purchase

Pharmacy

What is it?

ISO is known for its antiseptic qualities and is typically used in first aid or to clean skin before an injection. It can also be used to disinfect surfaces, reducing the risk of contamination.

Why use it?

The effective action of ISO is not in its application but instead in its evaporation. When applied, the alcohol soaks into the microorganisms that may contaminate a project. During the process of evaporation, ISO coagulates proteins, essentially turning contaminants into soup and killing them.

For the evaporative action to be completely effective, it is essential that you use 70 percent ISO. This is because 30 percent of the solution is water, the ideal amount to most effectively penetrate the microorganisms. At higher concentrations the alcohol coagulates the exterior, often leaving the contaminants still viable, and at lower concentrations it just won't pack the same punch.

Spray Bottle

Where to purchase
Pharmacy, big-box store, or salon supply store

What is it?
A plastic bottle with a spray attachment distributes ISO and other liquids evenly.

Why use it?
A standard spray bottle is fine for distributing ISO on surfaces, but the type of salon-style spray bottle recommended for spraying water in later phases of the project is even better. You may want to get two of those spray bottles now, and put away one for the later phases.

Lighter

Where to purchase

Pharmacy or big-box store

What is it?

Look for an ordinary, inexpensive cigarette lighter that is comfortable to hold, is easy to control, and has a steady flame.

Why use it?

A lighter plays an important role in keeping your project contaminant-free. You will use the flame to sterilize the needle of your spore syringe or liquid culture syringe before puncturing the rice bags. Since the needle is the only object actually entering the sterile bag, the flame helps to guarantee a higher level of cleanliness than alcohol alone would provide.

⚠ Warning

A lighter's primary purpose is to produce fire. Please go to great lengths to keep fire under control throughout your cultivation practice as ISO is highly flammable. The alcohol does not need to evaporate completely to be safe to work around, but it is best practice to wait for almost complete evaporation before using an open flame. Don't take any chances after spraying your gloves; wait until the alcohol has totally evaporated before progressing.

Pro Tip

While any type of lighter will work, some have a safety guard over the striker that can tear gloves. Here's a simple way to remove the safety and make the lighter mycologist friendly.

1. Insert a small metal object, like a key, into the hole where the flame comes out.
2. Lever the metal under the front of the safety and push it up, bending the small arms that hold the safety down.
3. Take the same piece of metal used for levering and place it between the back side of the safety and the striker.
4. Pinch the safety between the metal and your thumb and pull up while wiggling it back and forth. The safety should slide out with minimal resistance.
5. Bend the small metal arms that held the safety back to their original position.

Starter Culture: Spore Syringe or Liquid Culture Syringe

Where to purchase

inoculatetheworld.com

mycologynow.com

premiumspores.com

What is it?

Although you'll find a variety of potential starter cultures, they all come down to two basic options: spores or liquid culture (sometimes referred to as isolated syringes).

Why use it?

For a beginner, the best and easiest place to start is with either a spore syringe or a liquid culture syringe (see The Cultivation Life Cycle for more information). A syringe contains a sterile medium and makes inoculation simple and straightforward, removing many variables for the introduction of potential contaminants. To increase the odds of a contaminant-free syringe, choose one of the vendors listed here or another highly recommended and trusted source, of which there are many.

Pro Tips

Discretion. Spore syringes may not be illegal, but everything about their origin and typical use means that to stay in business, vendors try to stay on the right side of a blurry line. Because spores are sold for "research purposes" and not cultivation, it is best to roll with this intention and not ask the vendor about how well a certain strain grows or similar questions. It is not unheard of for someone to have an order canceled for implying an intent to cultivate mushrooms. The landscape is rapidly changing and these age-old traditions seem to be loosening, but it is advisable not to test them. Discretion is also wise when purchasing liquid culture syringes.

When ordering. When ordering starter culture, order more than one syringe if possible, so you have a backup. Syringes typically arrive in a nondescript box with a little stopper (sometimes referred to as a blunt cap) in the end of the syringe. You should also receive a needle, packaged in a sterile, single-use wrapper.

Storage. . Liquid cultures store reliably in the refrigerator for 12 or more months; spore syringes have a somewhat shorter lifespan in the refrigerator, 6 to 12 months. The best way to store a syringe is in a ziplock bag in the refrigerator—but try to use the syringe as soon as possible after receiving it.

Procedure

Quick Clean Checklist

- ☐ Clean the workspace.
- ☐ Gather your materials.
- ☐ Make the air in your workspace still for 15 minutes.
- ☐ Put on mask and gloves and disinfect your gloved hands with 70 percent ISO.
- ☐ Disinfect your work surface with ISO.
- ☐ Clean your materials with ISO.
- ☐ Spray ISO onto a paper towel and wipe the spray bottle first.
- ☐ Disinfect the lighter next so the alcohol has time to evaporate.
- ☐ Disinfect the rice bags next so that paper surgical tape or filter stickers will adhere.
- ☐ Disinfect the rest of the items in no particular order.

Preparing a Syringe

Breaking Up Clumps

While disinfecting the syringe body, take a close look at the contents. It is likely that the culture will be somewhat clumped. This can be more problematic with spores than liquid culture. If you notice any clumps, you have several options for breaking them up, but keep in mind that the syringe does not need to be clump-free. If some clumps remain after your efforts to break them up, that is okay. In the case

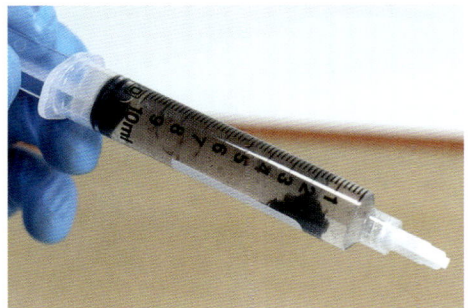

of spores, note that they are microscopic, so you can be sure that some of them will have broken away from the main clump and that you will be able to successfully inoculate your bags.

Your first option for breaking up clumps is to give the syringe a shake. If that does not work, try tapping it on your palm or against a firm but forgiving surface, like a plastic tub, cardboard box, or book. This method almost always works, although you may have to do it for a couple of minutes. If shaking and tapping fail, there is one more option: the air bubble method.

Spore Clumping

Spores have a characteristic that can be referred to as self-affinity, an almost magnetic attraction to themselves. This tendency often manifests as one big clump of spores in a syringe. A potential issue is that the clump might be injected all at once into a single rice bag. There will usually be some spare spores to grow in other bags, but growth in those bags will often be much slower. If you shake apart the clump, then the same amount of spores can be used in 10 or more bags.

Air Bubble Method

Attempt this method only in your fully prepared clean space, or preferably in a still air box (see the section Keeping It Clean). Pulling in air increases the risk of contamination, but only slightly. If you are mindful, there should be no issue.

1. Spray 70 percent ISO around the stopper on the syringe and let it evaporate.
2. Holding the syringe vertically, loosen the stopper so that it is almost

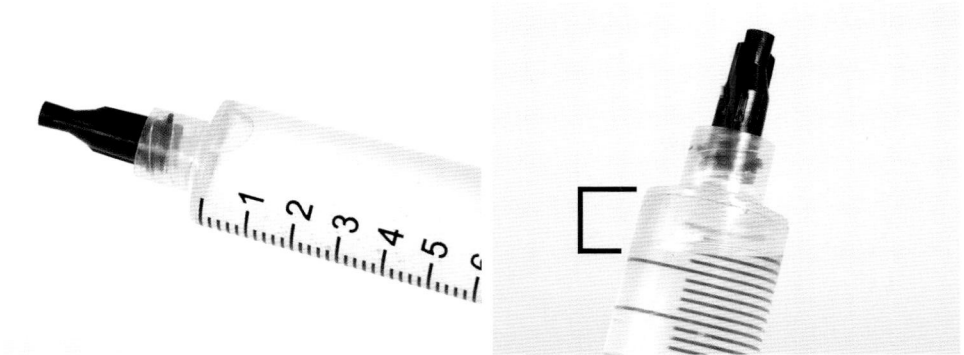

The air bubble does not have to be large to be effective, the smaller it is, the smaller the risk of any potential contaminant entering the syringe.

completely loose but still on top.

3. Still holding the syringe vertically, pull the plunger just a tiny bit to bring in an air bubble. It shouldn't be larger than 0.5 cc/ml.

4. Retighten the stopper and shake the syringe as hard as you can. This should do the trick.

Assembling the Syringe

With the culture well distributed, it is time to assemble the syringe. The first use of the syringe is to make some holes in the rice bag to serve as air vents. While inside their original packaging, the syringe and needle are sterile. Be careful when opening any sterile container and when handling a needle.

1. Hold the syringe vertically and loosen the stopper, but not so much it falls off.

2. Open the sterile wrapper containing the needle. The easiest method is to grip the needle firmly and tear it through the paper side of the packaging.

3. Quickly push off the stopper and place the needle with its cap on the end of the syringe. Twist clockwise to secure it.

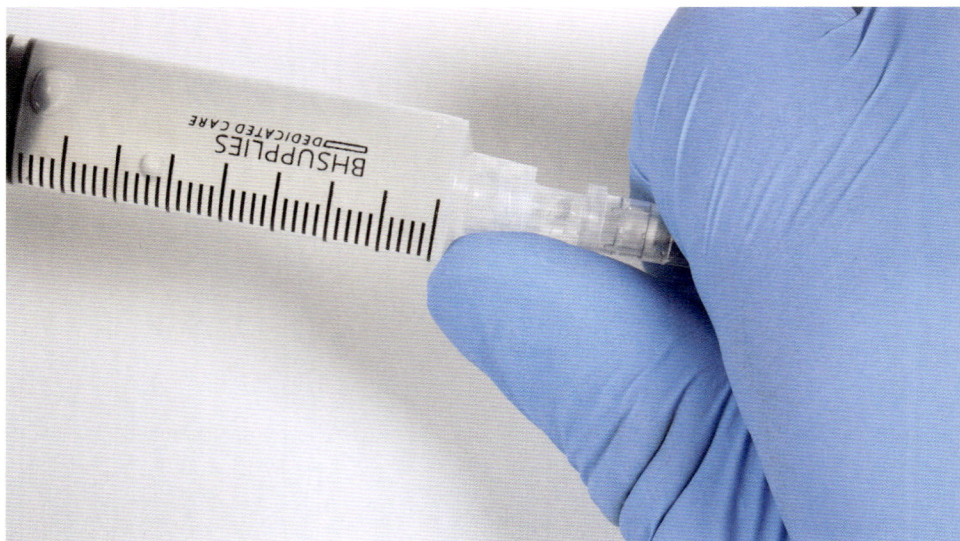

Removing and Reattaching the Needle Cap

Syringe needles are incredibly sharp, so be mindful when handling them. It doesn't take much for a needle to go into or through a finger (ouch!). The main moments of concern are when removing and reattaching the needle cap.

To remove the needle cap, firmly grasp the needle cap and syringe body in separate hands. Use the thumb on the hand grasping the needle to push the cap away from the syringe body. Slowly build pressure to just barely pop the cap loose, then remove it in a controlled manner.

To reattach the needle cap, hold the cap at the end farthest from the opening, carefully insert the needle, hold the needle somewhat vertically, and let the cap fall onto it fully. Snap the cap shut with modest pressure. Alternatively, you could scoop the cap onto the needle and snap the cap shut.

PRO

Pro Tip

Some cultivators like to replace the stopper when storing their syringe after use. This is not necessary and may introduce unnecessary risk; replacing the needle cap is enough for good storage.

Making Air Vents

Flame-Sterilizing the Syringe Needle

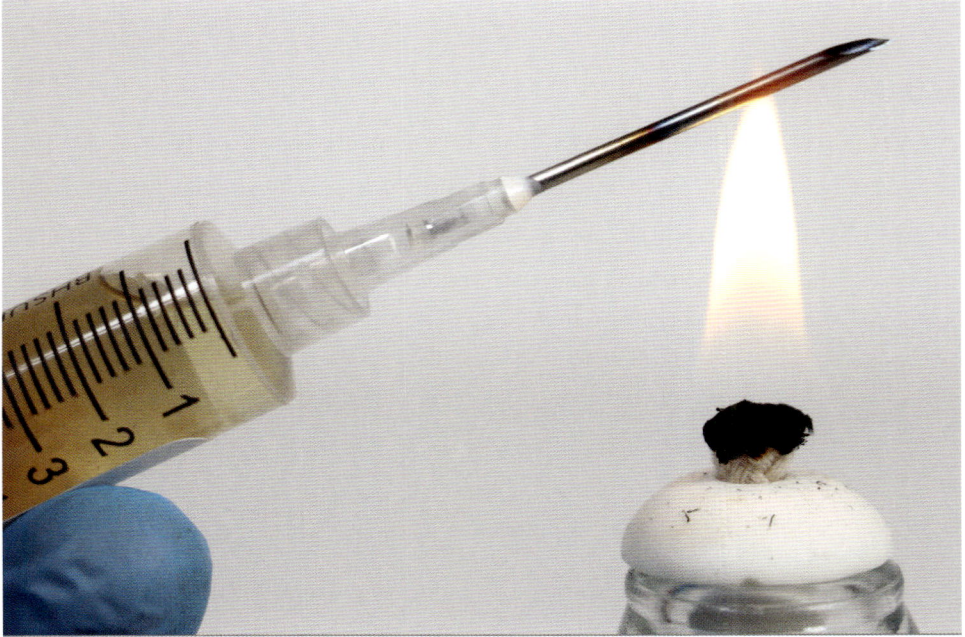

A brand new, just-opened syringe needle will be sterile, so there is no need to flame-sterilize it before its first use. Once a needle has been used, sterilize it in between uses when you move from making air vents to inoculating and when you move from one bag to the next. Here is a quick procedure for needle sterilization.

1. Holding your lighter in one hand, use your other hand to move the upper two-thirds of the needle back and forth barely above the hottest part of the flame, the tip, for 5 to 10 seconds. Avoid getting the flame too close to the plastic end or it may damage the needle.
2. Allow the needle to cool for another 10 seconds before using it. This will prevent it from melting the plastic and forming toxic fumes the next time it is flame-sterilized.

When no liquid is present in the needle, the metal will heat up very quickly. Heat it for about 5 seconds, and it will cool in about 10 seconds. After inoculation, when liquid is present, heat for 10 seconds and cool for the same amount of time.

Making Vents

Air vents in the top of the bag allow for gas exchange throughout the process of colonization (mycelial growth) and increase the speed of growth and health of the fungi. Getting air in the bag is also essential for the next step, injecting the starter culture. You can make vents by poking holes or using a hole punch.

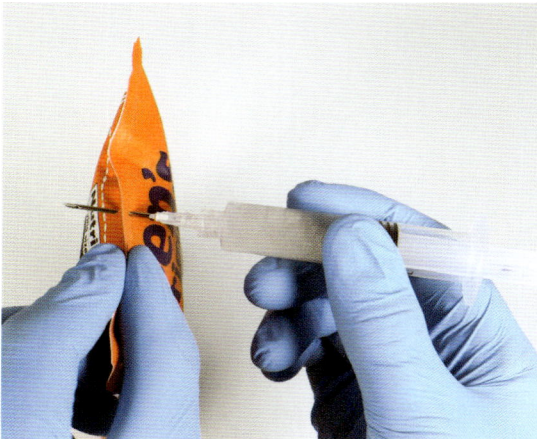

Poking Holes

Just below the plastic seal that goes across the top of the rice bag, use your syringe needle to make holes through both sides of the bag. Occasionally, rice is tightly packed all the way up to the seal. Gently guide any packed rice out of the way with little pinches before proceeding.

1. Be careful about your finger placement as you puncture both sides of the bag with the needle. Make a small cluster of 5 to 10 holes.
2. Keep an eye on both

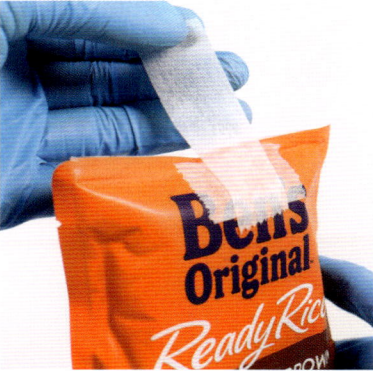

sides of the bag, to make sure that both the entrance and exit holes are staying in a small cluster. Holes so close together should gradually turn into a larger hole or two. If it looks like the holes are mostly separate, they are likely to seal themselves up when covered with paper surgical tape or filter stickers; take a few more stabs, then recap the syringe.

3. If using paper surgical tape (get rid of the exposed first inch or so if the tape is on a dispenser), use a piece long enough to cover the holes on both sides of the bag, going up and over the top of the bag. Then place another layer of tape on each side of the bag to cover the first layer of tape. It is good practice to place the second layer at a 90-degree angle to the first.

4. If using filter stickers like the ones offered by microppose.com, place one sticker on each side of the bag to cover the holes. No tape is needed.

Using a Hole Punch

This method using a one-hole punch follows most of the procedure described for poking holes, with some subtle differences. This method creates a more reliable air vent.

1. Prepare the hole punch by heavily spraying it or, even better, by submerging it in a small container of 70 percent ISO.

2. Allow the alcohol to mostly evaporate off the punch, then flame-sterilize the end of the punch for approximately 10 seconds. Any black carbon remaining on the punch is fine and doesn't need to be wiped off.

3. In the top center of the rice bag, squeeze the tool hard to make a hole through both sides. Sometimes the hole punch sticks in the shut position. Pry it open and remove it.

4. Tape up or apply filter stickers over the hole as described for poking holes.

Inoculating the Rice Bag

Ready   Before

Breaking Up the Rice

The vents will allow some air into the bag and make it easy to break up the rice. Massage the bag with your hands to break up the brick of rice. Tap the bag sharply on the working surface to dislodge any rice that has not settled into the lower half of the bag. The bag should be able to stand on its own. Feel around the upper edge to make sure no rice is trapped next to the seal; if there is some, gently guide it downward.

Injecting the Starter Culture

Now the rice bag is ready for spores or liquid culture. The scientific term for injecting starter culture is "inoculation," and in mushroom lingo you are inoculating grain or making grain spawn. Follow these simple steps:

1. Remove the cap from the syringe, and flame-sterilize the needle.

2. After letting the needle cool, position the syringe vertically so the tip of the needle is over the center of the bag about 1 inch above the "rice line," or where the rice has settled. Vertical positioning is important to avoid accidentally puncturing the back of the bag.

3. With your syringe in position, press down on the plunger to inject the bag with between 0.5 and 1 cc/ml of your starter culture into one spot. Don't spray it all around. Press carefully to avoid adding too much. Because the rice is already so well hydrated, excessive liquid increases the risk of contamination. Try to avoid touching the rice with the needle tip, as that can gunk up the needle.

4. Remove the needle from the bag and recap it. (When liquid is present in the needle after inoculation, expect some sizzling and popping as the liquid boils and steams away.)

5. Cover the needle hole with two pieces of paper surgical tape placed at 90-degree angles (as described for the air vent) or with a single filter sticker.

6. With a permanent marker, make note of the date, the mushroom strain, the type of starter culture, and perhaps a message of unconditional love and support. There's no conclusive science on the benefit of

an encouraging message, but it couldn't hurt.

7. Repeat this process for all the bags to be inoculated.

Waiting for Colonization

Protecting the Rice Bags

Once you have inoculated the bags, only a little bit of work remains: to keep the inoculated bags out of harm's way and in the right temperature range. The first consideration is finding a spot with still air and out of direct sunlight. You don't need a superclean environment or one with absolutely no air movement—just make sure there isn't constant air movement. Constant airflow increases the chances of a contaminant making its way through the paper surgical tape or filter stickers and may dehydrate the rice bags, slowing growth. A good example of a satisfactory location is a closet that might be opened a few times a day but mostly stays shut.

The second consideration is temperature. The optimal range for growth is 70° to 80°F. If you had to pick one number, 75°F seems to work for all strains of Psilocybe cubensis throughout their lifespan. Lower than 70°F and the speed of growth begins to slow. In the mid to high sixties, the speed of growth declines significantly; at those lower temperatures, growth often takes two to three times as long and may stall, meaning it could take more than 2 months for a rice bag to colonize, if it does at all. On the upper end of the recommended range, temperatures higher than 80°F slightly increase the risk of contamination. As the temperature nears 90°F, contamination has a much easier time gaining the advantage. At around 105°F, the health of the mycelium is at risk and growth typically slows; above this temperature, mycelial die-off is likely.

There is a wide range in which your mycelium can grow, and some fluctuations within that range are perfectly normal. However, the best results will always come by maintaining a constant 75°F.

Managing Temperature

If the space is cool, the easiest way to manage temperature is to colonize the bags in a walk-in closet using a temperature-controlled space heater with an adjustable thermostat. It shouldn't have to run much to maintain a constant temperature in a small space A thermometer next to the bags is helpful in adjusting the space heater temperature. Another advantage of closets is that they have still air and no direct sunlight. For safety, make sure to provide ample space around the heater.

In my time as a mycology educator, I've seen people throw away rice bags that don't seem to have progressed. Often the mycelium is just growing slowly, and the person didn't do a squeeze test to see if there was a problem (see Testing for Contaminants), and didn't break up the existing mycelium because it wasn't visible through the window. It hurts my heart when I see this, because typically nothing is really wrong with the bags, it's just that growth has slowed due to environmental conditions.

The less common reason for "no growth" is that the starter culture was dead. This is almost never the case, except for cultures that have been sitting around for too long or have been exposed to some kind of extreme conditions, such as direct sunlight, high temperatures, or freezing conditions.

The problem of "no growth" is usually an issue of slow growth because the temperature is too low.

Although people are trying to keep their utility bills as low as possible, frugal and fungal may find themselves at odds. If you are committed to growing your own mushrooms, then please also commit to maintaining optimal temperatures for the fungi. This means staying as close as possible to a consistent 70° to 80°F throughout the process.

Using an Incubator

If the space-heater-in-a-walk-in-closet method or other space with constant temperature and little air movement won't work for you, you have a couple of easy DIY incubator options that require a simple tool: a fully submersible, adjustable aquarium heater. This type of heater uses the mass of water to radiate heat at a consistent temperature, and it is inexpensive, usually only $10 to $20. Plus, it's far superior to and safer than a heat mat, which struggles to maintain as much consistency as an aquarium heater and can cause issues if not properly monitored.

Tub-in-Tub Incubator

One tub contains the water and aquarium heater, and the second tub, which is completely dry inside, contains the rice bags.

1. Get two of the same style of tub, preferably in the 40- to 60-quart range, that stack inside one another.
2. Add approximately 6 inches of water to the bottom tub, and turn the heater to a minimum of 80°F, although you will likely need to turn it up to maintain a consistent 80°F in the dry chamber. Most aquarium heaters have a built-in thermostat. Placing a thermometer inside of the tub will provide the necessary feedback to make any temperature adjustments to the aquarium heater.
3. Place the second tub inside the first. Put your rice bags inside this dry tub, and cover it with a lid. You can also throw a blanket or two over

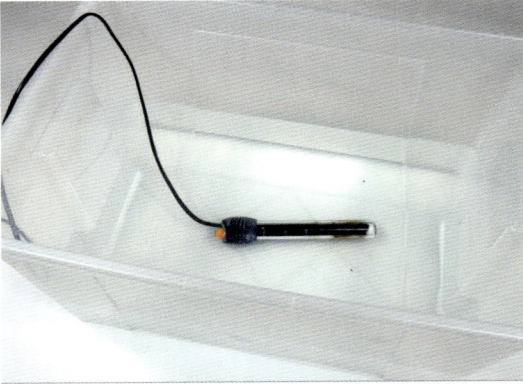

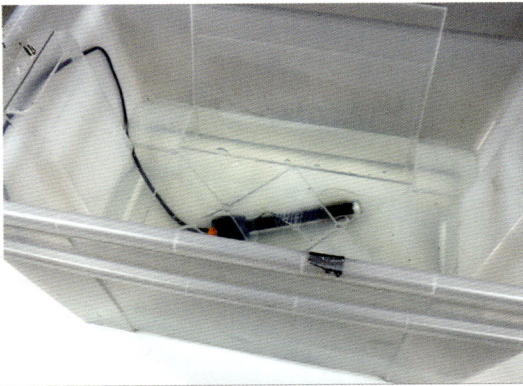

the top to insulate the tub and save energy.

In accordance with the laws of physics, the top tub will float on the water; the best option is to just let it float. If you want it to sink the tub slightly to improve the incubator by raising the heated water along the walls, add a couple of weights or fix the tub in place using duct tape.

Heat Bomb Incubator

An even simpler option than the tub-in-tub incubator is the heat bomb incubator. This method puts the aquarium heater inside a small loosely sealed (not airtight) container of water and then lets you figure out the best way to trap that heat in a small space. You could put it inside a cupboard or cabinet, a cardboard box, a large plastic tub, or a cooler.

To build the heat bomb itself, all you need is the aquarium heater and a lidded jar or bottle big enough for the heater to fit inside. A half-gallon mason jar may work, but use a larger vessel, such as a 5-gallon bucket, to heat a larger area. Place the aquarium heater and water inside the vessel, and close it up. The challenge with this method is the "close it up" part. Properly seal-

ing the top is recommended; otherwise, water will evaporate out of the vessel and into the incubation space, creating a damp drippy mess. Loosely fastening a lid or taping down a rubber stopper should do the trick. If using a mason jar, cut a small notch into the lid for the cord to stick out. Check on the water levels frequently to ensure the heater is always fully submerged.

A heat bomb gives you many options. One is to place the heat bomb inside a tub along with your fungi. Another option that works even better is to put the heat bomb along with your fungi inside a cooler. For fruiting later on, you would have to figure out a light source for the tub, but LEDs or Christmas lights would work.

Assessing the Mycelium

After about 10 days of colonization, there is often a good amount of growth in the rice bags—more growth with liquid culture, less with spores. You can do a couple of tests to see how far the mycelium has come along. When using liquid culture, 10 days can be nearly enough to finish colonization; spores generally need 14 or more days.

Visual colonization test. The easiest way to gauge colonization is to look in the window on the bottom of the bag. The downside is that, when injecting spores at the top of the bag, the spores may have a tendency to grow along the top, out of sight of the bottom window.

Touch colonization test.

The other way of gauging colonization is to gently squeeze the bag between a couple of fingers, not trying to break anything up but to feel for the firmness of the mycelial network binding the rice together. Start your exploration near the top where the mycelium generally begins. Mycelium growing between grains of rice creates a strong network of connections, so you should be met with a lot more resistance than if you just squeezed loose rice.

Breaking Up the Rice

After gauging the growth and finding that the mycelium is covering roughly 25 percent or more of the rice, it's time to break it up and redistribute the colonized grains throughout the bag. This will speed up colonization. If one bag is colonizing faster than the others, leave it alone until the others are ready. There isn't a big rush at this point, as colonized bags can remain viable for more than a few weeks. However, it is always best to use them when they are as fresh as possible. When your bags are fully colonized, you are ready for Phase 2 of your project.

Managing Contamination in Rice Bags

When the bags are first colonized, if you notice abnormal growth or coloring, there is nothing you can do except discard the bag and start fresh. It is sad but at least it's simple. Later in the project, when you move your project into tubs, undesirable fungal growth, typically green mold, is the most common issue, but bacteria and yeasts are relatively common contaminants in bags. You can identify them visually by their milky fluids or by rice that is off-color or mushy. Sometimes, you can identify them simply as an area where the mycelium grows around but never into.

Testing for Contaminants

There are three ways to test for contaminants inside a bag. If you use all three, you should be able to prevent 100 percent of contaminants from making their way to the next phase of your project.

Visual test. Given that many of the precooked rice bags on the market have a clear viewing window, it's easy to see if anything other than clean white mycelium is growing in the bag.

Squeeze test. This is like the touch colonization test to assess mycelial progress, but here you're testing for contamination. Healthy mycelium grows between grains of rice to create a strong network of connections. When you give the bag a light squeeze, you should be met with firm resistance, far different from the movement of loose grains of rice or something mushier. To my knowledge, no potential contaminant will mimic this type of density. If the contents of the bag feel loose or mushy, you'll know you have a problem.

Smell test. Give the bag a gentle squeeze above the mycelium to push some air out, get your nose close to the vented holes at the top of the bag, and take a whiff. You are likely to encounter one of a few scents. There might be something earthy, or mushroomy. This scent is a little hard to describe, but it is a lot like the smell you get when chopping fresh mushrooms from the grocery store. This is what you want.

Bad signs from the smell test are anything that stings the nostrils or has a rotten or overtly sour smell. Those are typically the scents of bacterial or yeast contamination.

Excess Liquid

Sometimes, excess liquid collects in the bottom of the rice bag. This tends to happen when the mycelium is fighting off a potential contaminant or with large temperature fluctuations. There may be other reasons as well. If this happens, take a close look at the liquid. Cloudy liquid is likely due to a contaminant. Clear liquid, even if it has a yellow, orange, or brown tint, is okay. Some people call it mushroom pee.

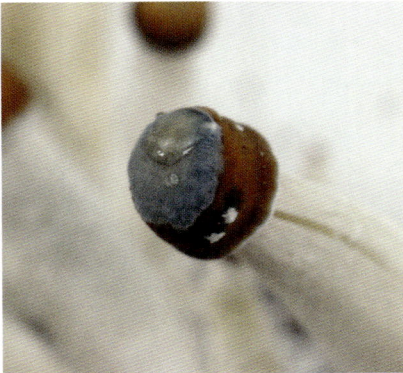

Top: The base of a recently harvested mushroom bruising an intense blue color. Some mushrooms are hollow.

Bottom: This strange growth is not mold but instead an area where the mushroom cap grew against the lid of the tub, began to produce mycelium, and said mycelium was bruised due to its contact with the lid.

Bruising

Bruising refers to discoloration of mushrooms that react chemically to rough handling. It shows as a bluish gray color, and you can rejoice in the fact that this blue bruising is a sign of psilocybin. When identifying bruising, take a close look and try to distinguish it as a color shift of the mycelium as opposed to another life form growing on top of the mycelium. If you can safely identify a bruise as opposed to contamination, then your bag is good to go.

Most people notice this phenomenon during harvest, when they are cutting the stems of the mushrooms. The most alarming (but less common) time that people notice bruising is when prepping their rice to mix with the substrate in the next phase of the project. Breaking up the rice can have a bruising effect on the mycelium, and this effect is usually more dramatic the longer you wait before mixing the rice into the substrate.

Phase 2: Colonizing the Tub

Materials

Checklist

- ☐ 6-quart shoebox tub
- ☐ Colonized rice bags (from Phase 1)
- ☐ Compressed brick of coconut coir
- ☐ Superfine powdered gypsum
- ☐ Vermiculite (optional)
- ☐ Flathead screwdriver
- ☐ Kitchen scale accurate to 1 gram
- ☐ 70 percent isopropyl alcohol (ISO)
- ☐ Two spray bottles (for ISO and water)
- ☐ Permanent marker
- ☐ Black trash bag for lining the tub (optional)

6-Quart Shoebox Tub

Where to purchase

Big-box store, home goods store, or hardware store

What is it?

The shoebox-size tub will be the home of your mushrooms. Make sure the container has clear walls.

While a clear lid is advantageous, it is commonly less available—an opaque lid will do just fine.

Why use it?

This type of small tub is the perfect container for the brand new cultivator. It is small, costs very little, requires no modification, and yet often produces upward of an ounce of mushrooms inside. It is also infinitely reusable and easy to clean. Because of the clear walls, light can penetrate and you can keep a close eye on the humidity level and watch the growth while opening the tub less often. Finally, if anything goes wrong in your first attempts, handling a problem in a 6-quart tub is easy.

Get enough tubs to accommodate all your bags of colonized rice; each shoebox-size tub will accommodate two bags. It's a good idea to get an extra tub for each tub of mushrooms you're growing, just in case you need to raise the ceiling (see the section Tall Mushrooms).

Compressed Brick of Coconut Coir

Where to purchase

Garden center or hardware store

What is it?

Aside from myceliated rice, hydrated coconut coir makes up the majority of what goes into the 6-quart tub. Derived

from the outer husk of the coconut, coir is often used as a growing medium for plants. There are two main types of coconut coir sold: loose and compressed. A compressed brick is the right choice for this project, as it is superdry and superabsorbent, which minimizes the risk of hitchhiking contaminants.

Why use it?

Coir is commonly used in the cultivation of psychoactive fungi because of its fluffy texture, high water-holding capacity, and natural antibacterial properties. While coir may have some nutritional value, it mainly provides optimal conditions for the rice-fed mycelium to produce mushrooms. You'll need one compressed brick for every tub of mushrooms you're growing.

Superfine Powdered Gypsum

Where to purchase

Gypsum is available at some garden centers and hardware stores, but finding the correct variety, superfine powder, is not always easy and may be sold only in large quantities. Since you need only 1 tablespoon per tub, try checking a brewing supply store or online for small quantities.

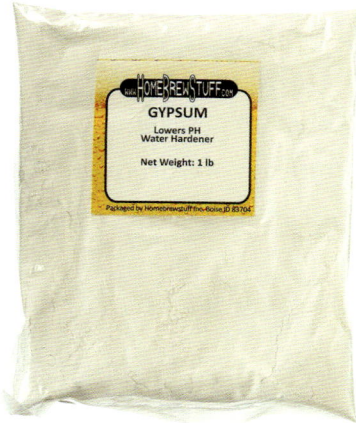

What is it?

A fine white powder, gypsum is a calcium and sulfur amendment that you will stir into the coconut coir.

Why use it?

Gypsum is reputed to boost the potency of psilocybin mushrooms. Although the actual effect of this boost is up for debate, it is still the most common amendment in mushroom cultivation—and until the data proves otherwise, cultivators keep using it.

Vermiculite (Optional)

Where to purchase

Garden center or hardware store

What is it?

Vermiculite is a lightweight, silvery gray mineral with a spongelike quality commonly used in soil mixes and for growing seedlings. The fact that it is mined is a deterrent to some people. Vermiculite has a habit of cre-

ating a lot of airborne dust when it is poured and moved around, so be sure to wear a dust mask when working with it.

Why use it?

The main purpose of vermiculite, similar to coconut coir's purpose, is to provide moisture and aeration to the substrate. Also like coir, it is resistant to contamination. While vermiculite, often shortened to "verm," is unnecessary, it holds more water than coconut coir and contributes to larger flushes of mushrooms, typically yielding as much as 10 to 15 percent increase in production over multiple flushes when used at about 20 percent by volume of the substrate. You don't need vermiculite to cultivate mushrooms; it's of modest benefit in dry climates. Use it in a ratio of 2 parts vermiculite to 1 part water.

Kitchen Scale Accurate to 1 Gram

Where to purchase

Big-box store or home goods store

What is it?

Most food scales have the features you'll need for this project—accuracy, an easy-to-read screen, the ability to switch between different measurement units, and the ability to tare (reset to zero).

Why use it?

You'll need to combine ingredients with precision, and a common kitchen scale accurate to 1 gram allows you to do it. Scales come in a range of prices, and you may find one for less than $15.

Spray Bottles

Where to purchase

Pharmacy, big-box store, or salon supply store

What is it?

A spray bottle described as a salon spray bottle, hair spray bottle, or continuous mister spray bottle, which produces an ultrafine, continuous mist, is ideal for adding moisture throughout mushroom cultivation.

Why use it?

Two spray bottles are optimal—one for distributing 70 percent ISO, although this can be done with an ISO-soaked paper towel, and the other for misting the mycelium and the interior of the tub with water. A standard spray bottle is adequate for distributing ISO, but a finer spray is necessary for misting water. It's worth seeking out salon sprayers for both functions. Label the bottles with a permanent marker, so each is reserved for a specific use.

Tap Water or Clean Water

What kind of water is suitable for misting the mycelium? Luckily, no special water is required, and you are welcome to use whatever you prefer and is available. Just be sure the water isn't obviously dirty or contaminated. Any water that is good enough to drink is good enough for growing mushrooms.

Procedure

Lining the Tub, or Not?

Lining the sides and bottom of the tub with a piece of plastic bag (typically, a black trash bag) is optional, but it provides a benefit for not too much extra work. The liner helps prevent side pins, or mushrooms growing on the sides and bottom of the cake as opposed to the top, where you want them. Additionally the liner helps retain moisture within the cake and prevents it from sitting in stagnant water.

Side-pinning, in part, seems to be determined by genetics. It may be the case that some strains produce few or no side pins whereas others want to grow primarily in that zone. Liners cannot prevent this issue entirely and it is best to change genetics if side pinning persists.

I have personally grown many more tubs without liners than with them. Although I get slightly better results when using them, I have often opted to skip the extra step and the small amount of single-use plastic. Still, I am a proponent of liners and recommend trying both ways.

How it works. The liner works in two ways. First, it sticks directly to the substrate, which prevents air and moisture from contacting the edges of the cake, making the lined area less desirable for pin formation. Second, the liner blocks some light, which discourages healthy pin formation. Ideally, the vast majority of mushrooms will grow on the top of the cake, as lining creates less desirable conditions for growth on the sides and bottom.

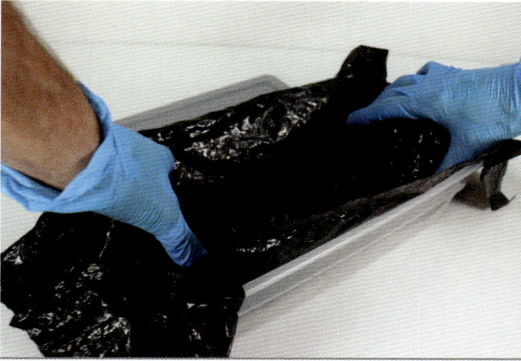

How to make it. Trim a black trash bag into a size that fits the tub—a 12 x 16-inch piece is ideal for a shoebox-size tub. The easier way is to trim an oversized piece of plastic after placing it in the tub and adding and leveling the ingredients. Spraying the inside of the tub first with a thin layer of 70 percent ISO helps the plastic stick to the tub. The best tool for trimming is a small razor. Scissors also work well enough. When using a razor, avoid scratching the inside of the tub as deep scratches can harbor contaminants during future use.

Overview of Next Steps

❑ Break up 155 grams of compressed coconut coir.

❑ Place the coconut coir in the 6-quart shoebox tub and slowly hydrate it with 775 grams/ml of boiling water.

❑ When the coir is fully hydrated, add 1 tablespoon of powdered gypsum and mix thoroughly with a disinfected utensil.

❑ Click or lock the lid in place, and allow the mixture to slowly cool for 6 to 12 hours.

❑ Test the hydrated coir for field capacity by squeezing it lightly.

❑ Add the colonized rice, break up the clumps, and flatten the surface.

Preparing the Substrate

Breaking Up the Coconut Coir

Breaking up the brick of coconut coir can be one of the most challenging parts of the project, but not if you know how to approach it. Notice that two sides of the brick are pretty flat with no texture, but the other sides, typically the shorter edges, have lengthwise striations. The trick is to get into the striations using a flathead screwdriver, to take the brick apart. Here's how to proceed:

1. Place the brick on a cutting board to avoid damaging the work surface when the screwdriver goes through the coir.
2. Insert the screwdriver into and through the striations. It's easier to start close to the edges rather than dead center.
3. Use a scale to measure 155 grams.
4. Use your hands to break apart the large pieces into nickel- and quarter-size pieces. Smaller pieces hydrate faster and more evenly.

Boiling the Water

The next step is to pour boiling water on the coir. Although this is often referred to as pasteurization, it is not truly pasteurization, but is close enough. For 155 grams of coconut coir, use 775 grams (equivalent to 775 ml) of water—that's a ratio of 1 part coconut coir to 5 parts water. Boil water for one tub's worth of coconut coir at a time. A kettle may be the safest and most convenient tool, because the spout allows for deliberate pouring. When weighing the water for boiling, be sure to place the empty vessel on the scale and reset to zero before pouring.

Hydrating the Coir

Once the water is boiling, slowly pour it on the coir. You will get the best results by patiently going through the substrate and soaking each chunk of coir. Try to avoid water settling in the bottom of the tub as it will slow down or even prevent the even distribution of water. After pouring the water, let the tub sit until the coir fully absorbs the water.

Adding Gypsum

Once the coconut coir is hydrated, sprinkle 1 tablespoon of gypsum across the top of the coir and mix it in with a disinfected utensil.

While mixing, check for any remaining clumps of coir and break them up. Be sure to get down into the corners. Lift the tub up and check around the edges for homogeneity.

Testing for Field Capacity

Getting the ratio of coir to water just right is one of the keys to a great harvest, and while the provided ratio (1 part coir to 5 parts water) works quite well, you can't assume that it will work perfectly all the time. If you really want to go pro, it is not difficult to check the coir for field capacity, that is, optimal water-holding capacity. That means fully hydrated, but with plenty of airflow for all the microscopic hyphal strands of mycelium to quickly and efficiently navigate throughout the coir.

Test the coir by taking a handful and giving it a squeeze. Imagine a firm handshake that makes a good impression without doing any damage. A few drops of water should come out, but there shouldn't be a heavy stream. If the coir is too dry, just add some boiling water and mix it in until the moisture level is just right. If the coir is too wet, squeeze out some of the extra water and mix it back in until you are satisfied with the moisture level. If, at some point, you realize your coir is chronically dry, you can adjust your ratio of coir to water to a 1 part coir to 5.5 parts water or something similar. Chances are you won't have to adjust anything, but it's best to check the first couple of times to make sure everything looks good.

Adding the Colonized Rice

After the coir has cooled for 6 to 12 hours, check the temperature by feeling the outside of the tub. Probe with the thermometer or gloved finger to make sure the coir has cooled throughout. It shouldn't be much warmer than room temperature (75° F) before you proceed. A temperature higher than 95°F risks damaging the mycelium. Slightly warm is fine, but if you're uncertain, let the mixture sit a bit longer.

Once the coir is sufficiently cool, disinfect the rice bags with 70 percent ISO. Then massage the bags to break up the mycelium, and mix the rice into the coir. Put the tub back in its previous location, as long as it thrived there, to begin colonizing once again and ultimately fruiting. Here's the detailed breakdown of how to add the colonized rice.

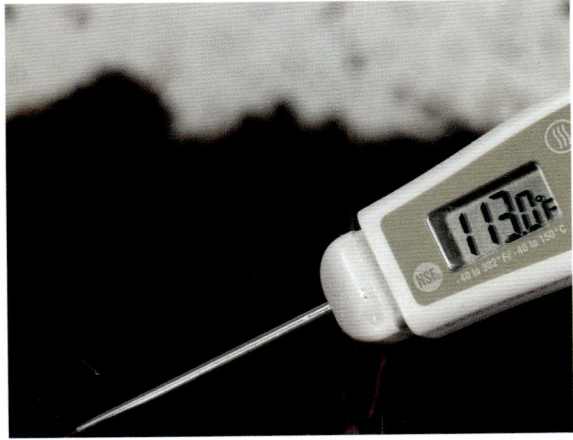

Left sitting, the mushier appearance of this rice is normal.

Breaking Up the Rice Bags

Prepare the rice by breaking it up again, much as you did in Phase 1, before inoculating the rice bag. Your goal is to squeeze, massage, and break up the clumps of rice into individual grains. The more you break it up, the more surface area, which correlates with faster colonization times and healthier fungal growth.

This rice has been broken up as soon as it was ready. When left sitting around longer, a mushier appearance can be normal.

Adding the Rice to the Coir

Cut or tear off the tops of the two rice bags for the tub you are working on. Even if you are working on several tubs at once, open the bags for only one tub at a time. Pour the colonized rice on top of the coir and mix it in with a disinfected utensil. Look closely at the sides and bottom of the tub to make sure that the mix is homogeneous throughout.

Flattening the Coir

Flatten, but don't compress, the top of the mixture with a disinfected utensil or gloved hand, leveling the surface and patting it down very gently. A flattened surface maintains an even microclimate of very humid air just above the surface rather than concentrating it into a few ravines. Imagine yourself shrunk down and standing on the surface of the coir; you want to look around and feel like you are in the middle of a huge field as opposed to hilly or mountainous terrain. Finally, mist water across the surface of the mixture and click or lock the lid into place.

125

Don't fear a bluish gray color. A bluish gray color is often responsible for good projects ending up in the trash. After breaking up the bags of rice, you might find that the previously white mycelium has turned bluish gray and assume that it's contaminated. In fact, it's almost always simple bruising. When the mycelium is handled roughly, the standard bruising reaction that happens with fruit also occurs with mycelium, creating the off-color. If you are not sure of the mycelium's health, smell the contents. It will smell bad if it's contaminated, stinging the nostrils with a rotten or sour smell, or it will give off a sickly sweet and lightly coconutty scent (a sure sign of green mold formation).

Waiting for Colonization—with Light

Return the tub to the same conditions that the rice bags succeeded in. The same temperature range (70° to 80°F) applies in Phase 2 as it did in Phase 1. There is one difference—light. It may be easiest to add light from the beginning, although technically it is necessary only after the mixture is fully colonized. In ideal conditions, tubs usually fully colonize in 10 to 14 days.

Mycelium does not require any light to grow, because it does so underground or within a substrate, but mushrooms do benefit from some light. They don't consume energy from light as plants do, but light encourages upright and healthy mushroom formation. Light also influences the direction of growth, meaning that light shone on only one side of the tub encourages the

mushrooms to tilt toward it and triggers more mushroom formation on that side of the tub.

Not much light is needed. A single low-wattage light bulb will do. With more light, such as a strip of LED lights, you will see healthier or at least more regular flushes. The light can be on for as little as a couple of hours a day, but some growers prefer a 12 hours on/12 hours off regimen. Other growers keep the lights on continuously with no detriment. A room that has ambient light from a window can also be used. Just keep the mycelium out of direct sunlight.

Maintaining the Tub

If you follow all the maintenance procedures and keep a close eye on your tub, it shouldn't be long before the tub is full of beautiful fungi.

Fresh Air Exchange

Colonization, or the time it takes for the mycelium to fully cover the entire surface of the cake, takes about 10 to 14 days. If full coverage doesn't happen in that time frame, just wait until it does. Once full coverage occurs, it is time to pop the lid, but don't remove it. Just unclip or unlock both ends, lift the lid up a little bit, and let it settle evenly back down. Popping the lid creates a tiny air gap around most of the lid, and this bit of extra air is all you need. While other voices may encourage more airflow, this technique works and additionally it decreases or even eliminates the need for misting to keep the humidity level optimal. Further increasing airflow is a worthwhile experiment, although it requires more attention to humidity levels.

Top Photo: Closed Lid. /Bottom Photo: Popped Lid

Flipping the Lid

Popping the lid works well, but if you don't mind extra maintenance for a potential payoff, flip the lid instead of just popping it. A flipped lid allows a lot more airflow into the tub, which increases evaporation and requires more misting to keep the cake from drying out. This process can

result in larger flushes. Evaporation from the top of the cake is the best way to increase the pin set.

Humidity and Surface Conditions

To properly maintain the tub, you have to keep a close eye on surface conditions, primarily the humidity of the cake surface. The ideal conditions occur when the whole surface of the cake and the tub walls are covered in a dense mat of individual supertiny droplets of water. Once these droplets have mostly evaporated from the surface, it is time for another misting.

It is possible to overmist the cake. You have overdone it when the tiny droplets of water begin to form larger puddles on the surface of the cake. This is not a big issue; absorb the water by dabbing it with the rolled-up corner of a clean paper towel.

Once pins begin to form, stop misting the cake and focus on misting the walls and the inside the lid. The misting and the evaporation cycle encourage primordia and pin formation, but after they begin to show, directly misting the cake is a leading cause of aborted pins. When you're misting only the walls and the inside of the lid, there will be overspray that gets on the surface of the cake. This is okay—just don't aim your spray at the cake.

How to Spray

The best way to achieve the perfect surface conditions is to use a salon-style or similar sprayer that emits a very fine pressurized mist and hold it about 1 foot above the cake. Spray in small bursts of 1 or 2 seconds, then wait a moment and spray again, checking the cake for coverage between sprays.

A standard spray bottle with a mist setting will also work. However, instead of directly spraying the cake, turn the bottle to spray into the air, allowing the mist to fall gracefully onto the cake. A distance of 1½ to 2 feet is usually enough for the spray to slow down and lose some of its initial pressure.

Signs of Humidity

A good way to know how humid or dry the cake is, and whether it needs misting, is to keep an eye on the tub walls. You should see the same type of tiny beads of moisture on the walls as you want to see on the cake. While checking the walls for moisture is a good rule, nothing is more important than actually looking at the surface conditions. Anytime the walls aren't mostly covered in moisture is a good time to mist them and or the cake.

Check tub walls and surface conditions for moisture.

Tall Mushrooms

Not all but many strains of mushrooms naturally grow tall. Often, they are very adaptable, accommodating their growth to the conditions provided, although they will readily push off a loose lid. You can help the situation by raising the ceiling. Instead of leaving the lid on and providing only a couple of inches for upward growth, take a second tub and place it upside down on top of the first tub. Line up the long sides of the two tubs, but offset the shorter sides by about ¼ to ½ inch. Use a single piece of tape along one of the long sides of the tub to hold the tubs in place; this also forms a hinge, allowing for easy access during harvest or for maintenance. Some cultivators refer to this as a dub-tub setup.

Watching for Growth

Once you start to see baby mush-room pins forming, keep a close eye on them because they grow fast. If you aren't careful, they can grow past their ideal time for har-vest. Also, be extra careful as the pins pop up, as they are sensitive to direct misting.

Phase 3: Harvest, Storage, and Continued Maintenance

Materials

Checklist

- ☐ Knife or scissors
- ☐ Ziplock freezer bags
- ☐ Food-grade silica desiccant pouches
- ☐ Dehydrator
- ☐ 70 percent isopropyl alcohol (ISO)
- ☐ Two spray bottles (for ISO and water)

Knife or Scissors

Where to purchase
Big-box store or hardware store

What is it?
A cutting instrument with a sharp blade is helpful in harvesting mushrooms.

Why use it?
While mushrooms can be harvested with or without a sharp blade, you'll want to remove the extra coir that inevitably sticks to the base of the mushrooms. Although either a knife or scissors will work well for harvesting mushrooms generally, scissors are better for removing stem butts when harvesting by hand.

Ziplock Storage Bags or Freezer Bags

Where to purchase?

Big-box store or grocery store

What is it?

Although standard ziplock storage bags will do the trick, freezer bags have multiple seals that further protect items inside the bag from outside air and odors.

Why use it?

With their multiple seals separating the inside of the bag from the outside, preventing air from entering the bag, ziplock freezer bags are a good, affordable storage option—with two caveats for long-term storage: include desiccants in the bags, and place each bag inside something else. While vacuum-sealed bags might be a better option for long-term storage, they are not a huge improvement on freezer bags (as long as the caveats are heeded), but are much more costly and require a little more labor.

Food-Grade Silica Desiccant Pouches

Where to purchase

Big-box store or hardware store

What is it?

Silica desiccant pouches are essential for dryness. You might know them as the thing you don't eat inside a bag of beef jerky or maybe you noticed them in a new pair of shoes. Because you will consume the mushrooms, you want a food-grade desiccant. The best type of desiccant to use with mushrooms includes color-changing beads, which indicate whether the desiccant is still absorbing humidity or if it is "full." Also, look for a desiccant product that is rechargeable in a microwave, oven, or dehydrator.

Why use it?

A silica desiccant prevents excess humidity from causing damage and can even make up for less-than-perfect drying. It works because it is extremely absorbent. You add the pouches to stored mushrooms to help maintain the driest environment possible.

Dehydrator

Where to purchase

Thrift store or big-box store

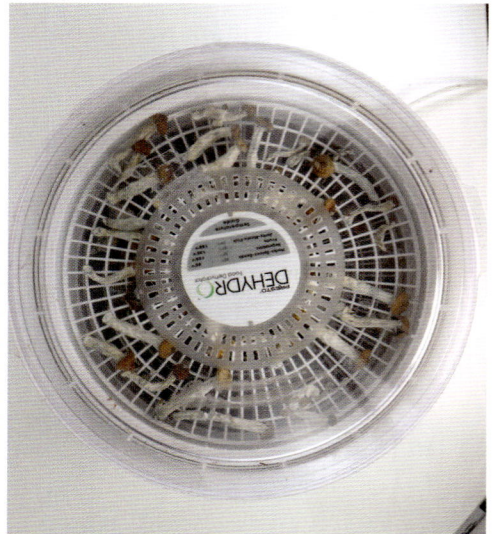

What is it?

There are many types of dehydrators with varying features, but all of them will do the simple job of making wet things dry.

Why use it?

Psilocybe cubensis mushrooms are about 90 percent water, and it takes a specialized tool to dry them quickly and effectively. The most beneficial features in a dehydrator are a fan that blows air and an adjustable thermostat that goes to 150°F or higher. It's possible to be successful with a model that has only a hot metal coil and passive airflow, but if you have a choice, get a model with a fan and adjustable thermostat. Ultimately, any kind of dehydrator is a good dehydrator, so don't turn down a good deal at the thrift store.

Box Versus Tray

Box dehydrators (including the popular Excalibur) are front-loading units with sliding trays. They are usually heated by a side- or back-mounted heating element that provides even heat throughout. They are very reliable. The limitations are that they are space hogs, offering no wiggle room for batch size, and are often more expensive than tray models.

Tray dehydrators are less consistent than box dehydrators. They are top-loading units with a base containing a heating element and sometimes a fan, a series of trays that stack on top of the base, and a lid that covers the top tray and closes the system. The greatest inconvenience of tray dehydrators is the narrow gap between trays that squish husky mushrooms.

PRO

Pro Tip

Solve the problem of a narrow gap between trays in a tray dehydrator by purchasing extra trays and removing the grate, essentially creating a spacer. This provides as much gap as needed for chunky mushrooms without squishing them while still allowing for good ventilation.

Procedure

Cleanliness

Although cleanliness in this phase is a lower priority than it was in the previous two phases, it's still important. Following the keep-it-clean guidelines discussed in Phase 1 is a good habit to get into.

Harvesting

The moment to harvest approaches quickly, but how will you know when it arrives? The right time to harvest is when the base of the mushroom cap begins to stretch out but hasn't fully opened. This narrow margin that connects the cap to the stem is known as the veil. Its job is to protect the gills until the spores are ready to spread. Harvest anytime this section is stretching but still intact, ideally closer to the beginning. The main benefit is that the mushrooms are more robust, staying intact throughout preservation and storage. When fully mature and open, the caps and stems often separate easily after

being dehydrated and the caps can easily break with rough handling.

The time between an ideal harvest and spores dropping can be as little as 8 to 12 hours. If you aim to harvest before sporulation and when the cap is still closed, you have a better chance of catching the perfect harvest window. If spores do fall, they won't affect edibility or further flushes; the mushrooms will just be messy and a little less beautiful.

Twist and Pull Method

With this simple method of harvest, you give a little twist before pulling, much as you do in picking most types of fruit. In the case of mushrooms, the initial twist breaks most of the mycelial connections around the base and the final tug easily breaks the remaining few threads.

The different strains of Psilocybe cubensis have varying degrees of connectivity. In some cases, even a properly executed twist and pull will leave a small crater in the cake. These craters are slightly problematic and may increase the risk of contamination and reduce pin production for future flushes. If you cannot twist and pull without damaging the cake, then use the cutting method.

Note that it is common practice to trim away the bottom or stem butt of the mushrooms when coir is still present before dehydrating the mushrooms.

Cutting Method

With this harvest method, a sharp knife or pair of scissors is used to cut the mushrooms from the substrate. The main thing that separates a good cut from a bad one is how close to the substrate you get without cutting into the cake. The problem with this method is that the pieces of the base left behind occasionally become contaminated. This is not usually a problem, but you should keep an eye on the bases because these are areas where molds may attack first, particularly on later flushes.

The benefit of cutting is that it is quick, leaves the mycelial cake intact, and gives you a mushroom with a cleanly cut base. However, getting a knife or scissors into the tub can be tricky. You may want to use both the cutting and the twist and pull methods.

PRO

Pro Tip

Once you've harvested your mushrooms, you can store them in the refrigerator for up to a week before using them raw or dehydrating them. If you're dehydrating, you may want to stockpile a larger batch of small daily harvests over a week and dehydrate them all at once. Expect to see some blue bruising on the mushrooms, especially along the stem.

Dehydrating to Cracker Dry

The chief factor essential in long-term preservation of mushrooms is dryness. The level of dryness you seek is as dry as possible, zero percent humidity. This state of optimal dryness is known as "cracker dry." You want the mushrooms to crack and shatter as opposed to bend and give. They should be completely brittle. If you are

able to achieve and maintain this level of dryness, then your mushrooms are likely to keep their potency for years to come.

There is plenty of debate about the best way to achieve cracker dryness, and the primary variable is temperature. Is it better to subject the mushrooms to low temperature over a long period of time or high temperature very quickly? Perhaps a middle path is the preferred way. Here are the best ways to get to cracker dry.

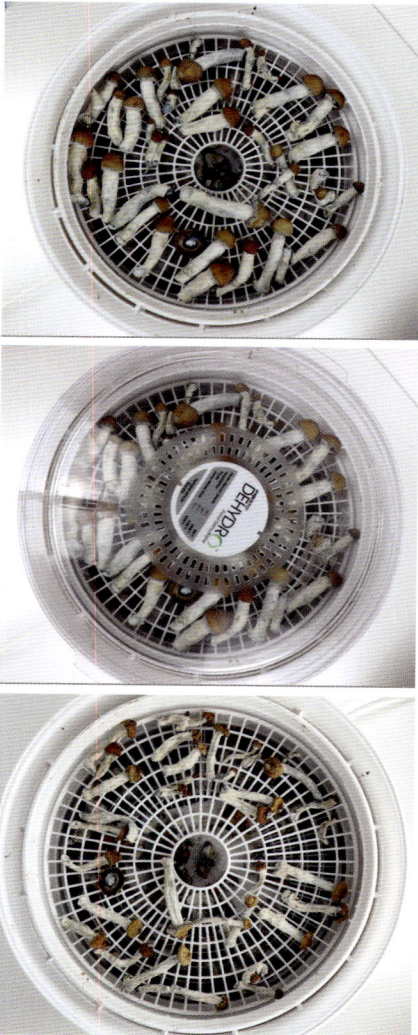

Dehydrator

The temperature I always opt for is 125°F. If you think that temperature is too high, feel free to go lower. Some people like to dry mushrooms at 100°F. It doesn't seem to matter very much. The only factor that seems essential is dryness. As for the argument that temperature affects potency, there is little to no data on the impact of temperature and drying time on potency; however, anecdotally lower temperatures do seem a little "safer."

At 150°F, the drying time is usually around 8 hours. At 100°F, it's closer to 24 hours. Drying time varies depending on the number of mushrooms and how large and dense they are, so check on them every 2 to 4 hours until they are cracker dry.

Be careful with drying too slowly. Drying that takes longer than a day is an invitation to harmful fungi and bacteria. Think of the harvested mushrooms as a food item; you wouldn't want a warm breeze blowing on beef jerky for a couple days before it finally dries out.

Fan and Oven

If you don't have a dehydrator, you can begin the drying process using a fan on the highest setting. This method takes at least 24 hours. If you have access to a drying rack or a similar surface that allows for airflow, use that as a base, propping it up on something to encourage airflow beneath. Then place it as close to the fan as possible and come back when it seems like the mushrooms won't get any dryer. Don't expect the fan to fully dry the mushrooms all the way to cracker dry. This is where the oven comes in.

Use the oven only when the mushrooms are as dry as possible but not cracker dry. Allow the oven to preheat to the lowest temperature setting, preferably lower than 170°F. Place the mushrooms on a cookie sheet or drying rack and into the oven. Check on dryness at least every 15 minutes. Remove the mushrooms when they are cracker dry.

The main problem with the oven method is the potential for damaging the entire batch due to the buildup of steam in the oven, especially if the mushrooms weren't fully dehydrated or the batch is large. You do not want to steam the mushrooms—they will turn a dark color and often become very hard.

Storing the Mushrooms

Principles of Long-Term Storage

- Mushrooms preserve their potency best when whole and not as powder.
- Airtight containers are best.
- Many containers considered airtight are not airtight.
- Desiccants are an absolute must.
- Multiple layers make up for a lack of airtightness.

Vacuum Sealing

A vacuum sealer that permanently closes the bags of mushrooms until their intended time of use is a great option. Include desiccant pouches in the bags before sealing. Seal small quantities, for example, 3.5 gram portions or perhaps enough for a batch of microdoses. Don't vacuum out all the air and risk crushing the mushrooms. It's more important to focus on getting the seal perfect.

Using Multiple Layers

Many people expect that finishing the job is as simple as putting the mushrooms in a mason jar and twisting the lid shut, or in ziplock bag and closing the seal. Mason jars are made for canning and are only airtight when the lid is vacuum sealed. And ziplock bags aren't airtight either. However, adding layers makes either of these options viable.

A bag inside a jar is better than just a jar, and a bag inside a bag inside a jar is even better. Of course, you can skip the jar and just use bags within bags. Ziplock freezer bags typically have the most layers of protection. Using multiple layers is still not at its best without a couple of food-grade silica desiccant pouches. Adding desiccant pouches into each layer of storage will leave your cracker dry mushrooms at their best for months or years to come.

Post-Harvest Care

Cleaning the Cake

Immediately after harvest, remove any fungal leftovers, including any aborted pins and tiny mushrooms, from the cake. To get at the sides and bottom, you can pop the cake out of the tub by flipping the whole tub over with the lid on. The cake will be upside down on the lid, and you can more easily

remove any funk before snapping the tub back onto the lid and flipping it back.

Focus mainly on fruiting bodies, that is, mushrooms that are growing, as they pose the greatest risk of becoming contamination vectors. You can clean up any little aborted pins, but they shouldn't cause an issue if you leave them. And don't forget to mist the cake very well before returning the tub to colonization conditions.

Quick Steps

- ☐ Remove any last little mushrooms or pins from the top of the cake.
- ☐ Flip the cake over onto the lid, exposing the sides.
- ☐ Clean up the sides and bottom of the cake and return to the original tub.
- ☐ Heavily mist the cake.
- ☐ Return the tub to colonization conditions and wait for another flush of mushrooms.

Continuing Harvests

You can expect multiple flushes from your mycelial cake. A flush is a wave of mushroom production. It may be hard to tell when your first flush is complete because mushrooms can still pop up here and there. However, after about a week of fruiting, the cake usually withdraws its energy from fruiting to prepare for a second flush. In some cases, third and fourth flushes are possible, and sometimes a well-maintained cake will continue to pop out a mushroom here and there for months to come. Still, the vast majority of mushrooms are produced in the first and second flushes.

With no further maintenance, the mycelial cake usually continues producing mushrooms. With a little maintenance, the health and abundance of subsequent flushes is much better. Water is the most critical component. Typically, a heavy misting—a dense coverage of moisture beads on the cake surface, the walls, and the underside of the lid—is enough to encourage the next flush. If your cake is a bit dry due to neglect or didn't produce a large first flush, a more intensive approach—a full soak—may help.

Further Maintenance

Once you have either misted or soaked your cake, the next step is as simple as keeping the cake in the same conditions in which it originally succeeded and also maintaining moisture throughout the process. Remember that as a mycelial cake ages, it becomes more and more susceptible to contamination and becomes less productive with every flush.

When to Move On

Your mycelium has colonized, it's reached its growth edges, and it has fruited. How do you know when it is time to move to the final stage of your mycelium's life cycle? Let's call this the burial stage, when you will return your mycelial cake to the earth. Ideally, you will have the opportunity to nutrify someone's garden or add to a compost pile. In any case, you will eventually get rid of the mycelial cake.

Typically, a spent mycelial cake has produced two or more flushes of mushrooms and has stopped production or has become overwhelmed by contaminants, usually green mold. The formation of patches of green mold after the second or third flush is perfectly normal and is a result of environmental contaminants taking advantage of the mycelium in a weakened state, when it has little more life.

Keep a closer eye than usual on the mycelium after the first flush, because when mold begins to spread it can do so at an alarming pace. When discarding moldy mycelium, do so away from your working spaces, in a well-ventilated area and quickly move it outdoors, to a compost pile or the trash.

What If Only a Few Mushrooms Grow?

What if your mycelium hasn't fruited or has produced very few mushrooms? Sometimes you go through all the steps and everything looks good, but very few or no mushrooms grow. If the temperature in your tub runs below the recommended 70° to 80°F, there will be a delay in colonization and fruiting. Also remember that 20 to 30 days until fruiting is a normal time span. If a delay isn't the issue, then there are typically two reasons for the lack of mushrooms.

The first reason is contamination. Take a close look and if you see anything besides mycelium, coir, rice, and maybe some pins, then your cake might be waging a war against contaminants. If you don't see anything amiss, then contamination is not the likely problem, as contaminants tend to be visible.

The second, more common reason for the lack of mushrooms is that the cake was too dry when initially spawning. The mycelial cake can have a relatively dry interior despite giving off the signs of healthy growth. If you have ruled out everything else, try putting your cake through a full soak.

Full Soak

Give the cake a prolonged dunk in water, fully submerging it. Once a common practice in mycology, increasingly a full soak as a regular procedure is going out of style. Think of it as more of a correction than a necessity. Here's what to do:

1. Find a spacer (any item that fills some of the gap between cake and lid) that you can easily clean with 70 percent ISO. It can't be a narrow object placed only on the center of the cake or it could break in half.

2. Before adding the spacer, clean the cake of all pins, aborts, and mushroom remnants. After cleaning the top, secure the lid and flip the tub over. Remove the tub from the lid as if the tub were the lid. Continue to clean the sides and bot-

tom of the cake in the same manner as the top. Replace the tub and flip it back to its regular orientation.

3. After disinfecting the spacer you have chosen, place it between the cake and the lid. Add enough water to submerge the cake by ½ inch or so, just enough so the top of the spacer sits just above the rim of the top, and lock the lid into place.

4. Let the cake sit for 6 to12 hours, then remove the spacer. Using a clean gloved hand, hold the cake as you drain the water, making sure you get every last drop. It's normal for the cake to take on the color of urine, so don't be alarmed.

As a Precaution...

Ordinarily, any drinking water is good enough to use in mushroom cultivation. But a full soak is one instance in which I like to use distilled or other pure water to recuce the risk of contamination. It's not necessary, but I don't like to take any chances with a full soak.

5. Return the tub to the spot where you had it previously and wait another 10 to 14 days for fruiting to occur. If nothing happens, it's time to start a new batch.

Recognizing Problems

Some growers are struck with anxiety about the appearance of their mushrooms, so here is a quick rundown of some situations you might encounter and how to handle them. Some things aren't a problem, but some are.

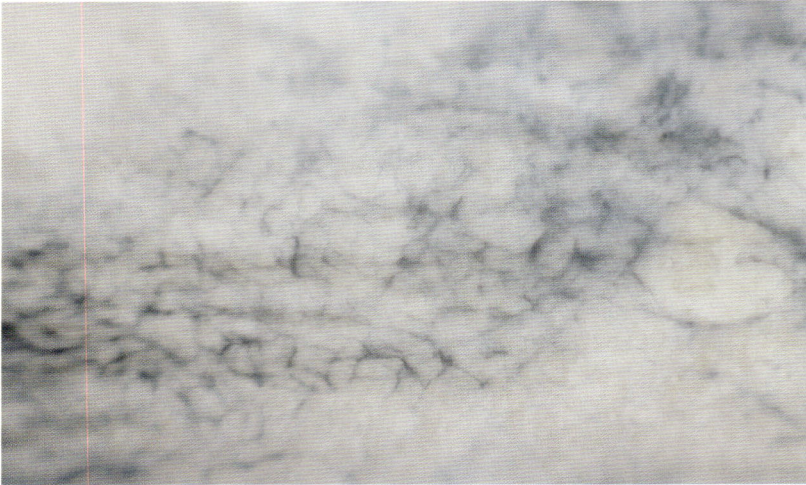

A close-up look of light bruising on a mushroom stem after harvest.

Bluing or Bruising: Not a Problem

Some damage to mushrooms is inevitable when harvesting them. The bruised areas typically turn blue due to the presence of psilocybin. This is not unusual and not a problem. Some theories suggest that more bluing correlates with greater potency, so if your mushrooms look like they took a serious beating after harvest, rejoice in the potential impact.

Fuzzy Feet: Not Typically a Problem

A white fuzzy or foamy-looking mycelium covers some portion of the mushroom's base. It might be the bottom ¼ inch all the way up to 1 inch and beyond. The first thing to know about fuzzy feet is that it is not contamination, but simply mycelial growth sometimes referred to as aerial mycelium. You may notice a similar phenomenon when your mycelium is colonizing the tub and little hyphal

branches poke straight up into the air.

Some people insist that fuzzy feet is a sign that carbon dioxide levels are too high and you should increase airflow. This is a fine instinct, and it may also increase the yield or size of your mushrooms, and some anecdotes suggest increased potency as well. However, fuzzy feet is not typically a problem and you don't have to adjust the airflow.

However, it's easy to increase airflow in a shoebox tub. The standard protocol is to pop the lid, but you can flip it instead. With a dub-tub setup (a second tub upside down on top of the first tub, allowing your mushrooms to grow taller), you align the longer sides on top of one another but leave a gap between the shorter sides. Both actions will improve airflow and reduce carbon dioxide levels—but the gaps will also reduce the humidity level, which means more frequent misting.

Clean Mushrooms, Contaminated Tub: Maybe a Problem

Even when a mycelial cake is highly contaminated, the mushrooms themselves may remain clean looking. In such a case, you may decide to use the mushrooms. The common belief is that if a mushroom looks okay, it is okay. If there is only a small patch of contamination, that is manageable and the mushrooms can be considered safe. If the tub is heavily contaminated, the best practice is to stay away from consuming any of the mushrooms.

Contaminated Mushrooms: Definitely a Problem

If you see any mold on the mushroom, then you should certainly discard it. See the section Discarding Contaminated Material.

Are Bacteria-Contaminated Mushrooms Salvageable?

Yellow or brown spots on the mushroom cap or stem, often referred to as blotch, are the hallmark of bacterial contamination. Blotch is a sign of too much humidity and or too little fresh air exchange. This type of contamination is most common when maturing mushrooms are heavily misted until they are visibly wet. It is an issue only if the mushrooms are consumed raw; blotch can cause mild food poisoning. When completely dehydrated, the bacterium that causes blotch is killed. Dehydrating at temperatures at or above 150°F ensures the destruction of the bacteria. If you're still worried, you can be sure of the organism's death by using the dehydrated mushrooms in a tea.

Managing Contamination in Tubs

Health Hazards of Common Contaminants

A big question for most new cultivators is, Are contaminants dangerous to my health? While the presence of molds typically is not serious, it can become serious at the crossroads of massive ambition and gross neglect. A single tub of moldy substrate is not a big health issue; you simply seal the tub, take it outside, compost or throw it away, and wash out the tub. You may wish to wear a surgical or N95 mask if the buildup of mold is particularly bad, because the spores are easily dislodged and can get into your airways. Even this situation is unlikely to impact your health unless you have a compromised immune system or asthma.

If you end up with many moldy tubs simultaneously, the risk of inhaling enough fungal spores to hurt your lungs and health does increase. It is for this reason that any cultivation projects should be taken with some of the same advice that goes for consuming psychedelic substances: start low and go slow. Start with a small manageable project that you can easily control before expanding your ambitions.

If you are keeping a close eye on your projects, it should be nearly impossible to end up with a large amount of mold. Just handle it as it comes; the more realistic problem is not your personal health, but instead the health of your cultivation space. The more contaminants that are left to sit around in your cultivation space, the higher the risk of future contamination. Of course, any space can be cleaned with some elbow grease and a modest bleach solution, but it's easy enough to avoid that situation. Just keep a close eye on your projects and handle contaminants as they pop up.

Dealing with Mold

Contamination in the tub can take a lot of forms, but the vast majority of cases are green mold. You may also see cobweb mold. Molds referred to as green mold are actually white, much like mycelium, but their spores provide the color we see. Cobweb mold is grayish white and looks a lot like mycelium. Most commonly, molds have a sickly sweet scent with a hint of coconut. While this can almost smell good, it is, of course, bad. By the time you have identified a mold problem, the organism is already spreading.

There are a couple strategies to overcoming mold. Quarantine is an option: shut the lid to seal off the potential spread and immediately remove the tub from your growing area. Advanced cultivators usually trash any tub with contamination, but new growers may find it hard to let go of their first project. Whether you can salvage your project depends on the number and location of contaminated areas. Removal is often the better option because of the threat of spreading the mold spores.

Just One Spot

If you see only one spot of contamination, then there is still hope. Using a disinfected tablespoon, scoop well around the contaminated area. Carefully transfer the scooped material in one intact piece to another container;

don't let any bits fall onto the cake. Start at the outer edges and work toward the center. Wipe the spoon with a paper towel soaked in 70 percent ISO after every scoop. Unless it's obvious that the contamination is limited to the surface (in which case, remove just the surface layers), continue tunneling down to the bottom of the cake.

Multiple Spots

Even if there are only two spots of contamination but they form simultaneously, the safe assumption is that the source of contamination was somehow mixed into the colonized rice. If you are lucky and the multiple spots are on the same side of the tub, then cut away a large portion of the colonized rice, keeping about 2 inches away from any contamination. Cut through the contaminated section with a disinfected knife, and use your gloved hands or disinfected utensils to discard the section. Once you've removed the contaminated area, dry the side of the tub with a paper towel, then disinfect the dry surface.

If the contaminated areas are at some distance from one another and are spread throughout the tub, then the advice is simple. Get rid of the tub contents as quickly as possible.

Discarding Contaminated Material

When discarding material due to mold problems, take precautions to minimize the spread of mold spores that can linger around your work area and increase the chances of future contamination. You may also want to wear a mask to avoid inhaling mold spores. Green mold and cobweb mold actually benefit plants, so you can simply throw the cake into the garden or onto the compost bin or pile. The least honorable option is the garbage. For discretion's sake, you may want to place the discarded material in a paper bag if you're discarding in a public place, such as a municipal compost bin.

Once you've discarded the contents, clean the tub with soap and water until it sparkles. Generally, soap and water are enough, but when mold has run rampant, a second round of cleaning with bleach is worthwhile. To be on the safe side, use a bleach spray on the tub, let it sit for a few minutes, and rinse it out.

Scaling Up Options

Premade Grain Bags

Most of the companies selling grain bags offer similar products, although seldom brown rice. Some of the most common grains sold are rye berry, wheat berry, oat, millet, and sorghum, but the most common by far is rye berry. These grains come presterilized inside an autoclavable (heat-resistant) bag with an injection port typically situated in the center of the bag. Additionally, the bags have a filter patch that allows for a tiny amount of gas exchange.

Premade Substrate Bags

If you also want to skip preparing your own substrate, you can purchase premade substrate. The most common is CVG—a blend of coir, vermiculite, and gypsum. This is a common substrate for new growers and differs only slightly from the coir and gypsum substrate recommended for shoebox cultivation. The primary alternative is a manure-based substrate or a CVG substrate with manure added. The most common manure-based substrates use horse manure; other options are typically referred to as "exotics."

Starter Culture

As you scale up, you will quickly realize the financial impact of purchasing new cultures again and again. With a few new skills and small investment it's easy to go from culture consumer to culture creator. Here's how to turn one liquid culture syringe into a lifetime of fresh inoculant.

Making Liquid Culture

Materials Checklist

- ❑ Modified lids
- ❑ Mason jars
- ❑ Sugar source (such as table sugar, honey, corn syrup, or light malt extract)
- ❑ Agitator (stir bar or marbles)
- ❑ Stir plate (optional, for stir bar)
- ❑ Large pot
- ❑ Starter culture (liquid culture syringe, fresh mushroom, mycelium on agar)
- ❑ Tweezers or scalpel (for fresh mushroom)
- ❑ 10 ml syringes and 16 gauge needles
- ❑ Still air box (optional)

Modified Jar Lids

While store-bought mason jars are used as is, a wide variety of modifications can be made to their lids, creating sterile containers for media preparation. For liquid culture, modified lids feature an air vent for gas exchange and an injection port for liquid extraction. These lids are available online or standard mason jar lids can be modified at home.

Premade liquid culture jar lids. Types are available for both wide- and narrow-mouth jars.

Partial DIY. Order filter stickers and injection port stickers from micropose. com. Carefully drill two ¼-inch holes in the jar lid, ½ inch from the raised lip, directly across from each other. It is safest to simply do this while the lid

Steps to making your own Liquid Culture Broth.

is adhered to the jar. Apply a filter sticker over one hole and an injection port sticker over the other hole to create a DIY liquid culture jar lid for much less than you'd pay for a store-bought version.

Agitation

Stirring the liquid culture breaks up the mycelium and promotes mycelial growth; it also makes extraction with a syringe much easier. There are two common methods of agitation:

Marbles. This affordable method involves adding two or three marbles to the jar before sterilizing it. You swirl the marbles to create a vortex.

Stir bar and magnetic stir plate. This more effective method uses a stir bar (added to the jar before sterilizing) and magnetic stir plate to agitate at a high rpm and break the mycelium into very small pieces. It is now more affordable thanks to reduced prices on scientific equipment.

Simple Liquid Culture Broth Recipe

Liquid culture broth is essentially sugar water. Many varieties of sugar will work; honey, corn syrup, light brown sugar, and light malt extract powder (my favorite) are popular choices. Dry sugars are far easier to work with and measure accurately.

1. Place the empty mason jar on the scale (tare, or reset, to zero), then add the desired amount of water. Fill about half the jar when using marbles and as much as two-thirds when using a stir bar.
2. Use the water weight to calculate the quantity of sugar to add. You'll need 2 to 3 grams/ml of sugar per 100 grams/ml of water.
3. Add the preferred agitator (marbles or stir bar).
4. Place the modified lid on the jar, and cover with aluminum foil.
5. Sterilize the jar in a pressure cooker or with steam on the stovetop.
6. Allow the vessel to cool naturally without releasing the pressure or opening the lid.

Sterilizing

Electric pressure cooker sterilization. Although an electric pressure cooker, such as Instant Pot, is generally easier to use than an old-fashioned stovetop pressure cooker, its pressure cook setting reaches only around 12 psi. For best results, increase the time to 45 minutes. Place a nonmetallic trivet or other item in the bottom of the pot to prevent the jars from touching the metal and cracking the glass. Fill the pressure cooker with water halfway up the jars. After running, allow the jars to cool overnight and open the pot close to your workspace for maximum cleanliness.

Steam sterilization. Fill the pot with water halfway up the jars, and use a trivet or similar item to protect the bottom of the jars. Sterilizing liquid culture with steam takes 60 minutes at 212°F (boiling temperature), so place a tight-fitting lid on the pot and begin the countdown after steam starts to vigorously escape the pot from under the lid. Allow the pot to cool before removing the jars.

Inoculating

Inoculate the broth with 1 to 2 cc/ml of liquid culture. Maintain the inoculated jar in an area with relatively still air and no direct sunlight and where the temperature is 70° to 80°F. Agitate the jar for 30 to 60 seconds every 3 to 7 days to increase mycelial growth until growth stops.

Filling a Syringe

Set up a clean workspace, agitate the mycelium to break up clumps, disinfect the jar and lid with 70 percent ISO, and use a needle and syringe to extract the liquid culture. Make sure to flame-sterilize the needle if it has been used before.

Managing Contamination

To minimize the risk of contamination, test new liquid culture by inoculating an agar plate or a single rice bag. If you detect contamination, dispose of the contaminated liquid culture, for example, by pouring it into garden soil.

Spotting contamination. Distinguishing between good and bad growth in liquid culture can be challenging. Mycelial growth looks like clouds suspended in clear broth, while contaminated growth causes the entire broth to become cloudy.

Storage. Clean liquid culture will stay that way for a long time and be usable for a year or more. It is best stored in the refrigerator for long-term use. Length of storage is not typically a reason for contamination, but the number of extractions from the jar increases risk. If a jar is being used frequently, it's a good idea to run a small test bath before doing extensive inoculations.

MYCORISING

Learn More With Seth

In addition to writing this book, the author is also the founder of MycoRising, a community building and education initiative based in the San Francisco Bay Area with a national impact. He leads weekly "hikerodoses" (hike+microdose), teaches classes on psilocybin use and cultivation, and supports individuals through their microdosing journeys one-on-one.

Continue Your Journey Online With Free...

RESOURCES
CONNECTION
SUPPORT

MYCORISINGFUNGI.COM/BOOK

Thank you to these companies for their support for the mushroom community.

WHOLESUN WELLNESS

www.wholesunwellness.com

CANADA
Chaga

UNITED STATES
Alaska, Colorado, Florida, and Utah

Chaga	Oyster
Cordyceps	Reishi
Lion's Mane	Shiitake
Maitake	Turkey Tail

SCOTLAND
Lion's Mane
Maitake
Oyster

INDIA
Lion's Mane
Reishi
Shiitake

THAILAND
Blazei
Cordyceps
Poria

SIBERIA
Chaga

JAPAN
Maitake
Reishi
Shaggy Mane
Shiitake

NORTHERN CHINA
Black Fungus
Poria
Tremella
Turkey Tail

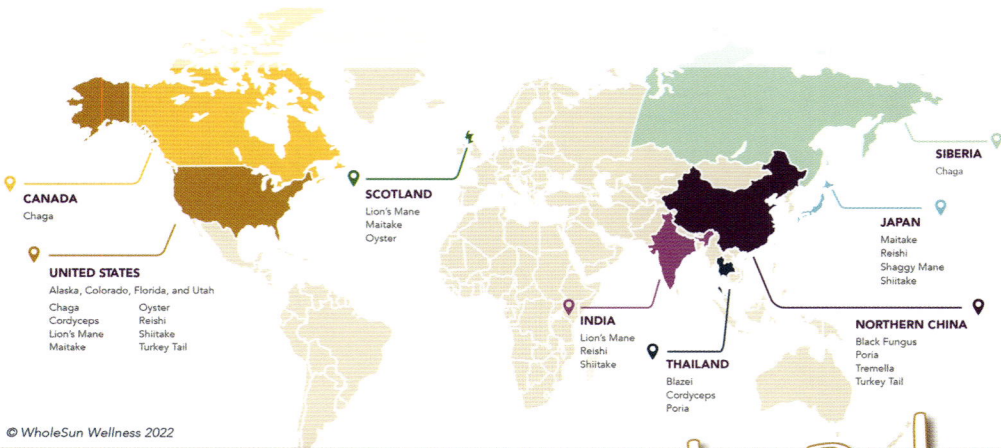

© WholeSun Wellness 2022

DO YOU KNOW WHERE YOUR MUSHROOMS COME FROM?

WE DO!

TRANSPARENT
We test our mushrooms beyond the industry standards for quality, purity, potency, and nutritional value.

TRACEABLE
We track every batch of mushrooms and are the only mushroom company to vertically integrate and source from U.S. farms.

TRUSTWORTHY
We build direct and exclusive relationships with our growers across the globe so we ensure each mushroom is grown to our high standards.

wholesunwellness.com

A HIGHER STANDARD FOR MEDICINAL MUSHROOMS

USDA ORGANIC · UDAF · ÖKO-GARANTIE BCS · ECO CERT · VEGAN · GLUTEN FREE · NON-GMO · aLita Bioscience Quality Testing

Discover the power of ancient knowledge

In the 1970s two of the most influential thinkers of the psychedelic era **the McKenna brothers** gathered what was then known about psilocybin botany and culture and presented it in **Psilocybin: Magic Mushroom Grower's Guide**. Writing under pseudonyms, the McKenna brothers provided simple, reliable, and productive methods for magic mushroom propagation. **Scan the Code and go down the rabbit hole** www.edrosenthal.com

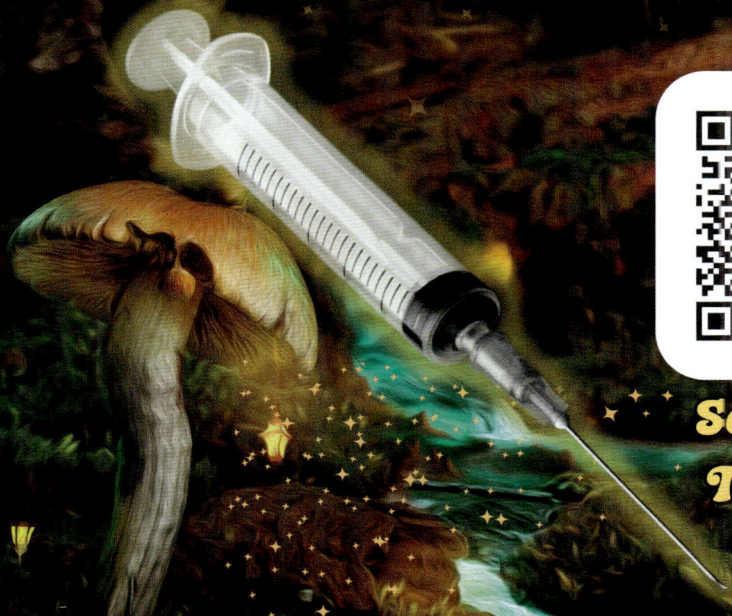

Notes

Notes

Notes

Notes

Notes

Notes

Notes